TALES
of the
ALASKA STATE TROOPERS

TALES

of the

ALASKA STATE TROOPERS

Stories of Courage, Survival,
and Honor from the Last Frontier

Peter B. Mathiesen

Skyhorse Publishing

Skyhorse Publishing books may be purchased in bulk at special discounts for sales promotion, corporate gifts, fund-raising, or educational purposes. Special editions can also be created to specifications. For details, contact the Special Sales Department, Skyhorse Publishing, 307 West 36th Street, 11th Floor, New York, NY 10018 or info@skyhorsepublishing.com.

Skyhorse® and Skyhorse Publishing® are registered trademarks of Skyhorse Publishing, Inc.®, a Delaware corporation.

Visit our website at www.skyhorsepublishing.com.

10 9 8 7 6 5 4 3 2

Library of Congress Cataloging-in-Publication Data is available on file.

Cover design by Rain Saukas
Cover photo provided by Peter B. Mathiesen

Print ISBN: 978-1-62636-068-6
Ebook ISBN: 978-1-63220-145-4

Printed in the United States of America

Dedication

To my wonderful family, who have endeared the woods and
rivers, always lending their unfathomable support.

Thank you, Sandra, Michael, Bekah, Hannah, Zach, and Bailey

A Special Thank You

There have been two people in my life who have encouraged me to tell stories.

A special thank-you to my dear wife, Sandra, and my mentor, Slaton L. White.

I would have starved without you both.

Contents

Acknowledgments

Many individuals assisted with this book with everything from referrals to research and even flying me to the bush.

Thank you to Tom Anderson and the FOAST organization; Tom and Renae Redman; Gary Peters; Sheila Selkregg; Deb Brock and KTNA; Marilyn Wick; Mat and Aurora Courtney; Tom and Janet Lemmon; Jenny Kreppel; Tony Martin; and the Public Affairs Office of the Alaska State Troopers.

And a special thank-you to Shani, who hijacked a dinner with a great suggestion, and Jay Cassell for his patience.

Introduction

Alaska State Troopers, like all law enforcement officers, are willing to face tremendous responsibility and risk. Yet, there is one key difference in the Last Frontier: these men and women in the forty-ninth state are frequently covering territories the size of Massachusetts or larger.

The troopers are assigned to five geographic detachments that provide patrol, enforcement, and search and rescue to all areas of the state. There are no county police departments and only about a dozen municipal departments. Their call of duty covers sixteen boroughs and their entire state employs an average of 419 troopers who cover an area nearly three times the size of Texas. Their territory includes a handful of highways, a few paved roads, and countless, winding gravel and dirt roads. And in rural Alaska, these troopers are the only law a citizen can call.

During the winter, troopers respond and work in some of the deadliest weather on the planet. Their dedication is utterly remarkable. They're driven by their passion for their jobs, for adventure, for the love of their state, and for a pledge to the oath they've taken to protect that state's unique citizens. They face incalculable risks with fearless commitment in the face of a fully armed populace—often with no assistance. On any given day, they could face a rogue bear, an unstable armed resident, a drug dealer, a smuggler, a terrorist, or even an errant moose.

They use floatplanes, helicopters, jet boats, ATVs, snow machines, airboats, and yes, even the occasional cruiser. You would find these men and women obsessed with unswerving dedication along with a deep admiration for the state they serve.

During the interview process, it became apparent that although these stories are truly remarkable, they are commonplace among most troopers. Many rural troopers have found unexploded ordnance or dynamite, scraped a frozen body off the floor of a remote cabin, or had to move a thousand-pound moose off a lonely stretch of road—alone.

This book chronicles just a few of the stories that were told to me personally by the Alaska State Troopers who participated in and witnessed these events. They are true and not exaggerated. And, in a place as wild and untamed as Alaska, the circumstances make these behaviors seem typical. Yet, they would be atypical anywhere else in the United States.

History of the Alaska State Troopers

Highway and rural law enforcement is a challenging job anywhere. Even in the western United States with large expanse and lonely roads, most State Troopers know what it feels like to be alone with no backup. However, in Alaska, a State Trooper faces challenges that can't be equaled by any other state in the lower 48. One-fifth the size of the contiguous United States, Alaska comprises 586,412 square miles of extraordinarily diverse territory and climates that are life-threatening even in the summer.

State Troopers cope with blizzards, hundreds of inches of snowfall, avalanches, winds in excess of 100 mph, sub-zero temperatures, and heavy rainfall. The state has more inhospitable vertical terrain than anywhere on the continent, with endless mountain ranges, glaciers, tundra, and rainforests. There are more than 3,000 rivers, more than 3 million lakes and a coastline of 6,640 miles. The vast expanses of the state often possess more danger than the traditional form of violence associated with a law enforcement career.

The evolution of law enforcement in Alaska began in the mid-1800s when the United States Army and Navy was the sole law enforcement authority throughout the vast region. Later, United States Marshals were appointed but were far too few in number. The tumult of the Gold Rush period, both at Skagway and Nome, first brought to focus the need for an additional law enforcement organization to supplement the US Marshal's Office. However, the US Marshals would continue to bear the responsibility for law enforcement in Alaska for the next forty years.

By the early 1950s, the Federal Department of Justice recognized the increasing law enforcement needs of the Territory, particularly in the bush areas of Alaska. The Territorial Legislature responded in 1953 by establishing the Alaska Territorial Police to provide law enforcement services for the entire Territory. Total strength: thirty-six officers. The Alaska Highway Patrol had already gained a reputation as an elite corps, and formal training became a hallmark of the new Territorial Police. As the officers began to serve in remote posts, they gained a reputation for integrity and capability, a reputation that has been carried forward to the present day.

With the advent of statehood in 1959, the name of Alaska's law enforcement agency was changed to the Alaska State Police and the organization became a division of the Department of Public Safety. The new State Police added thirteen former US Marshals and ten new recruits to their ranks, increasing their number to seventy-eight commissioned officers. During this time, the State Police would provide "contract officers" for communities willing to pay for trained law enforcement. Kotzebue, Kenai-Soldotna, Seward, Palmer, and Bethel were among the communities to pay for a contract officer from the State Police.

During Governor Wally Hickel's first administration in 1967, the name was changed to the Alaska State Troopers. Under Commissioner Mel Personett, the troopers focused their work in areas of Alaska not being served by community police and offered more sophisticated services to law enforcement organizations statewide. Also in 1967, the Public Safety Training Academy saw its first year of operation.

Today, the Alaska State Troopers number approximately 240 commissioned and 190 civilian personnel. The major components of the Division are: the Alaska Bureau of Investigation, which investigates major crimes and enforces bootlegging and illegal drug distribution throughout Alaska; Judicial Services, which is responsible for prisoner transports and providing security for Alaska courts; and the Alaska Bureau of Highway Patrol, which keeps Alaska's highways safe by their presence on state roadways and through public education campaigns. The detachments are headquartered in Ketchikan, Palmer, Anchorage, Fairbanks, and Soldotna.

You may visit the Alaska Law Enforcement Museum in downtown Anchorage at any time.

The Alaska Law Enforcement Museum
320 West 5th Ave
Anchorage, Alaska 99501
907-279-5050
www.alaskatroopermuseum.com
Admission: Free

* *Special thanks to FOAST and the Alaska State Troopers for this historical information.*

The Trapper Creek AMC Eagle

The call came into the Talkeetna sub station where it was forwarded to Trooper Dan Valentine's voice mail. The Trapper Creek caller made a special request: "I need to talk to Wildlife Trooper Dan Valentine. Don't send me a Blue Shirt; I want a Brown Shirt," he said. The trooper was off duty, but had checked his voice mail that afternoon.

After listening to the message, he phoned his lieutenant to see how he should respond to the caller. "Go see him. He has given us great information in the past, and he's quite the character," said Valentine's superior. He called the man back and told him he would come by sometime the next day.

Trapper Creek rests at Milepost 115 off the Parks Highway, two hours north of Anchorage and less than three hours south of Denali National Park. The town is two miles across the Susitna River from Talkeetna, although there is no bridge linking the two villages. Gold and the building of a rough wagon road brought people to the Trapper Creek region. In 1905, gold was discovered in the Cache Creek mining district some forty-five miles west of the Susitna River. In 1917, the Petersville Road served as a supply station to the gold-mining operations still active at the end of the Petersville Valley, fifty miles to the northwest into the interior.

The crossroad town of just fewer than five hundred consists of a gas station/campground/motel, a gift shop/DMV, a pizzeria/

bakery, a post office, an eclectic museum, petroleum services, and a cultural gifts store known as Wal★Mikes. Much of Trapper Creek enjoys sweeping views of the Alaska Range with staggering vistas of Denali. Not a touristy town, its populace is known for being remarkably independent with many living a subsistent lifestyle.

It was early May, a time when Alaskans are excited by the prospect of summer. Although at times immersed in melting snow and sloppy roads, sunsets start to linger past 10:00 p.m. around this time.

After catching up on some paperwork and teaching a boating safety class at the Talkeetna Elementary School, Trooper Valentine headed north up to the Parks Highway. Within twenty minutes, his Ford F250 pickup truck was sliding down a greasy road to the end of a grass airstrip at Mile 3.5 on the Petersville Road. He concluded the four-wheel drive would need to be parked, and he hiked the last five hundred yards. He saw a man driving toward him on a mud-soaked snow machine on the boggy road. The time was about 2:30 p.m.

The landowner, nicknamed Gator, was a classically gritty Alaskan bearded man who wore soiled Carhartt insulated work clothes. He greeted the trooper in a comfortable manner: "Thanks for coming out. I needed a Wildlife Trooper. I have something to show you." They rode back to Gator's house on the snow machine in the mud, never touching any snow.

The caller's home was an old Alaskan Railroad worker bunkhouse car that had been converted into a makeshift dry cabin. A door and a few extra windows were installed with the help of a blowtorch and were sealed with spray foam insulation. The car used a wood stove for heat, and by most accounts, would have been considered austere. It certainly wouldn't meet any neighborhood association's approval in the Lower 48. Abandoned cars circled the railcar, along with a few vans, railroad hardware, and a single maroon 1980s AMC Eagle station wagon. The wagon was parked fewer than seventy-five feet from the railroad domicile. The autos had remained parked since the 1990s when the property owner had run an impoundment and tow service for the Troopers.

The trooper surmised that, since the man had been a big game guide in the 1970s and he had assisted the troopers in several poaching cases, he was more comfortable talking to a "Wildlife" Trooper than a regular "Blue Shirt" Trooper. After a discussion about a firearm that was taken five years ago from another call with a different trooper, he brought Valentine's attention to another matter.

"I'm getting concerned about this, and I'm not sure what to do," said Gator.

The two walked over to the AMC, and the property owner requested the trooper look inside. "I'm not sure exactly what that stuff is made of, but I don't think it's safe," he said, his tone nonchalant. Trooper Valentine peeked through the twenty years of accumulating dirt smudged on the window and he could see a blanket with some stacked material underneath in the far back of the Eagle.

"Can I get inside?" asked Valentine. With a calm affirmation from Gator, the officer lifted the handle of the tailgate to find out that it was locked. "You mind if I break this lock?" After another calm approval from Gator, the trooper put his duty boot on the bumper and jammed his Leatherman utility tool into the keyhole. After a few kicks from his boot and hits of the folding tool, he vigorously shook the back of the vehicle until his Leatherman broke off in the keyhole.

"Well that's not ideal," he said under his breath, knowing he had just broken a brand new sixty-dollar folding tool.

Gator then spoke up and said, "I think the driver's door is unlocked." They walked a few steps in the twenty-four inches of wet-packed melting snow, and the trooper opened the door with ease.

"I'm not sure what influenced me to be more cautious, but I grabbed a stick to lift up the blanket," recalled Valentine during our interview.

When the trooper raised the blanket, he could see a collection of oval tubes tied end to end. A gelled liquid oozed out of the paper seams and some of the tubes had crystals growing on the ends.

"Hmm," he said. "Mind if I take one out?"

With a long reach forward, he pulled one of the tubes out and read HIGH EXPLOSIVES on the package. He took a photo with a digital camera and gently put it back.

"I knew it was an explosive, I just didn't know it could be unsafe. We really don't have any training to deal with these circumstances," he explained.

After gently lowering the blanket down, he asked the resident what he thought the packages were if he knew where they had come from.

Gator had evidently purchased the railcar from a local person who bought several from the State when it sold equipment from the Alaska Railroad. It was unclear if the railcar was completely full of these packages or if the only explosives on the property were the approximate 550 pounds in the Eagle. Gator told the trooper he had no idea the explosives were in the rail car when he purchased it.

In 1983, President Ronald Reagan signed legislation authorizing the transfer of the Alaska Railroad to the State of Alaska. When the federal government divested the railroad to the State, thousands of items, from railcars to scrap iron, were sold to the public in private sales and auctions throughout the following years. The hardware can be seen in villages strewn throughout the state as storage bunkers, and frequently, as in this case, housing.

"I'm just figuring that the stuff might be dangerous, and I have no idea what to do with it. I thought you guys could tow it away or burn it. Maybe you could blow it up for some kind of training. That would be a good thing, right? I was going to use it for either gold mining or maybe to clear a pit to keep buffalo in," Gator announced proudly with a sense of purpose. "Why don't you take some back to the office to show your boss?"

The sense of trepidation started to grow within Valentine. Call it intuition or heightened awareness, but he thought it was time to gather more information and he politely declined the offer to take some back to the Substation.

After clarifying these were the only explosives left on the property, Valentine told Gator, "I need to make a few calls. I know 'the Troopers' don't have anyone to deal with this, but I'll be right back."

He walked off through the woods and mud back to his truck.

Now completely caked in mud, the trooper called dispatch and asked, "Do we have a number to call for an EOD (Explosive Ordnance Disposal) Team?" Evidently, it was not a call the dispatcher received with any frequency; however, after a minute or two, Valentine was given a number for the EOD unit in Metro Anchorage.

When a sergeant picked up the phone in Anchorage, Valentine explained the circumstances, including the estimated five-hundred-pound weight of the explosives, the script on the packages, along with the condition of the tubes, including the leaking and crystallizing.

The APD sergeant asked, "How far are you from the Eagle?"

Valentine responded, "About a quarter of a mile."

The Anchorage sergeant immediately responded, "You need to double that, right now."

Just then, Gator was running the snow machine toward the truck. Valentine stepped out and said with a sense of urgency, "We need to move, now! You can't go back home. It's not safe."

Gator was amused by what he believed was a joke. "What? Are you kidding me? What the f— do you mean, I can't go home?"

After a convincing conversation, Valentine backed his truck up a half mile and Gator followed on his snow machine. While this was going on, the trooper was still connected on the phone with Anchorage EOD. The sergeant told Valentine he was going to make a few calls and call him back.

The trooper's phone rang a few minutes later and it was an officer, one of the EOD specialists at Fort Richardson Army Base, which was part of Joint Base Elmendorf-Richardson (JBER). The base borders the Anchorage city limits on the Glen

Highway. "This sounds pretty bad, but all of our gear is packed and we'll be shipping out to Afghanistan tomorrow. Listen, call the EOD team at Elmendorf. Here's the guy's number."

Valentine immediately called the Air Force number at the neighboring base and reached the EOD team. After hearing the story, the Elmendorf officer was highly concerned and wanted to deploy a team to the site immediately. However, there was one problem. "We can't operate outside of an Air Force–sanctioned assignment on public soil without at least the oversight of the FBI. I'll call you right back."

With that, Valentine observed that Gator had grown decidedly more agitated and less cheerful with every phone call the Trooper made. Valentine reiterated he could not return to the railcar.

"Okay damnit, I'm going to get my mail." With that, he jumped into his pickup and headed to town in the opposite direction.

With all the information at hand, the trooper called his commanding officer in Palmer, one hundred miles away, and explained the circumstances. He was told to keep him informed and call back the moment the FBI contacted him. In the meantime, they would send an additional trooper from Willow, about sixty miles away.

Minutes later, Valentine's cell phone rang. It was the FBI. They were sending two bomb technicians from Anchorage. The EOD team from Elmendorf had also been deployed. Their ETA was approximately two hours by vehicle. About that time, Trooper Terrence Shanigan arrived, and the two troopers evacuated a few of the closest homes.

When they finished the evacuations, they encountered a makeshift emergency vehicle parking lot on the Petersville Road as numerous personnel descended on Trapper Creek. The Techs from the FBI arrived first, and then the EOD team from Elmendorf gathered at around 8 p.m.

Additional troopers had also been assigned to help with further evacuations and traffic control. A Red Cross shelter was set up at the nearby elementary school, just outside the two-mile evacuation circle. Several fire and rescues units arrived from Talkeetna, Willow, Big Lake, and Wasilla up to eighty miles away. The EOD and FBI personnel strategized about the possibility of moving the Eagle to a gravel pit just one mile away for a safe detonation.

As they suited up in their bomb gear to go in and assess the situation, Valentine noticed Gator had returned and was carrying a twelve-pack of beer. More perturbed than when he left to get the mail, he yelled at Valentine: "Why did you call the Fed Man? This is a State problem!"

The trooper confiscated the beer and asked Gator to calm down. He told him they would know something soon. Minutes later, the troopers, with the help of a local pastor, removed Gator, who was now screaming, and put him up in a room at the Trapper Creek Inn and Gas Station four miles down the road.

When the EOD team returned from the site inspection, they determined the explosives were fifteen to twenty years old and included ammonium nitrate and nitroglycerine. "This is really bad . . . I'm not kidding. We can't move that Eagle an inch. Hell, if you were to just step on the bumper, it could easily blow! A small earthquake could set it off! We're going to blow it right where it sits," said the senior Air Force EDO tech.

Valentine wasn't sure if he should feel sick that he almost orphaned his family, or lucky that he and Gator were still alive. However, it was apparent everything the homeowner currently called his own in the railcar and yard was in serious jeopardy of being instantaneously destroyed.

The phone and radio traffic reached a fever pitch. One of the trooper's helicopters had been dispatched to the site to look for anyone within the possible blast radius with infrared vision.

Emergency personnel had now swelled to more than seventy-five persons with numerous ATVs to get to cabins not accessible because of the deep snow and mud. An ambulance team even removed a bed-ridden elderly woman since her home was considered to be inside the blast radius.

As the EOD team prepped the twelve-pound charge to be used as the detonator, and while an all-clear for a two-mile circle around Gator's home was being declared, another call came in. This call was to alert the team that Gator's permission had to be secured to blow the car.

Assisted by another trooper, Valentine drove to the Trapper Creek Inn to see Gator and to receive permission on tape to blow the Eagle. "It wasn't a very comfortable moment, and we were definitely considerate of his feelings. We felt genuinely bad for him. But, clearly, he knew there was no going back home with 550 pounds of nitroglycerine parked next to his bedroom," said Valentine.

During May, Alaskan daylight gains an average of more than six minutes a day. The call came in eleven hours earlier at 2:30 p.m. and it was now past midnight with twilight finally turning to near darkness around 1:00 a.m.

With Gator's permission recorded, and an estimated two hundred residents out of harm's way, the area was ready for detonation after 1:30 a.m. A final, infrared-viewing flight of the helicopter provided a last all-clear as the ground support people readied for the blast.

Valentine huddled with three other troopers in a patrol car. "We were instructed to make sure all the glass was rolled down, and if we had eye protection, to wear it. With my ATV goggles on tight, I waited for the detonation. The first thing we noticed was a bright flash. Just about the time I thought this was no big deal, the shock wave hit the car with a vengeance, rocking the heavily sprung Ford multiple times. There was debris in the air, and the sound was intense."

Not a single resident of Trapper Creek was unaware of the explosion. Valentine said his sister fourteen miles away on the Talkeetna Spur Road awakened thinking it was an earthquake. Fire crews quickly checked for ground flashes, and the EOD team verified the entire cache of nitro was completely destroyed. Valentine went to the Inn, where he found Gator now engulfed in whiskey and inebriated beyond reasonable communication.

He was in no condition to be allowed back to the site until later that morning.

Once the all clear was given, residents headed back to their homes, and Valentine headed home for some rack time. In the morning, he headed back to the site to complete the follow-up interviews and assess the damage for his report.

Once back on the site, several fire rescue personnel and a few troopers were still finishing up. Valentine got an eyeful of what 550 pounds of nitro can do to a yard full of cars and trucks. The first thing he noticed was the lack of snow. Gator was cleaning the glass up in the rail car and, to everyone's amazement and relief, the railcar was actually intact. However, all the glass had been destroyed.

The blast had completely removed the five-thousand-pound Eagle without a trace . . . gone. The van parked next to it and the car parked on the opposite side were relocated twenty yards. All that was left were the frames. All engines and body parts were missing. Because the heat from the explosion had melted the frost under the surface, a four-foot deep and thirty-foot wide hole had formed in the ground and was full of muddy soup. There were car parts littering the nearby woods up to three hundred yards away. Yet, no whole engine parts from the Eagle were found.

As for Gator's neighbors, their wooden structures didn't fare quite as well as his steel boxcar. Several dozens of windows were blown out and shattered. In addition, a few doors were dislodged and one home suffered a cracked foundation. One resident more than a quarter mile away reported a massive oval-shaped crease in his garage door.

In the coming weeks, Gator got his place back in relative order while receiving visits from multiple federal and state agencies inquiring about the rest of the explosives in the original freight car. However, at the time when the railroad equipment was purchased, it was not illegal to possess or sell the explosives.

The impressive irony is that the explosives were sold by the State of Alaska as the owners of the Alaska Railroad. No charges were filed. Although Trooper Valentine promised his wife he would never shake an automobile full of explosives ever again, he did find one memento of the AMC Eagle: the Eagle's license plate had landed two hundred yards away in the woods. The mangled, but intact, Alaska plate rests on the trooper's desk. It serves as a reminder to be more cautious the next time he encounters an abandoned vehicle. Because, in Alaska, you never know what's inside.

Two years later, on November 22, 2012, Gator (Calvin Hutchinson) died in a fire of undetermined origin in the same railcar that survived the blast. He was sixty-eight years old.

When I met Trooper Tage Toll, as described in a later chapter, we briefly discussed this event and he revealed that a resident had informed him Gator had hidden a large jar of gold under or inside the AMC Eagle. Toll said, "It was no wonder he so agitated during the detonation." No gold was ever found on the site. Unfortunately, I was never able to speak about this further with Trooper Toll. He perished in a helicopter crash just a few days later.

Hell Hath No Fury Like the Dalton Highway

Built during construction of the Trans-Alaska Pipeline System as a supply route in the early 1970s, the James W. Dalton Highway is also known as Alaska Route 11, or the Haul Road. It stretches 414 miles across northern Alaska, crosses the Yukon River and Arctic Circle through the rugged Brooks Range, and travels over the North Slope to the Arctic Ocean. From the Livengood turnoff of the Elliott Highway, 84 miles north of Fairbanks, to Deadhorse, it winds north across the tundra to the Arctic Ocean where the sixty-foot-wide gravel-caked roadbed ends at the oilfields of Prudhoe Bay.

Made famous in the reality television genre and often referenced in *Ice Road Truckers*, it is one of the most remote roads in the world. The highway, which runs directly parallel to the pipeline, is one the most isolated roads in the United States. There are only three towns along the route: Coldfoot at Mile 175, Wiseman at Mile 188, and the town of Deadhorse at Mile 414 on the bay.

In the late seventies, Fairbanks was in classic Alaskan boom and bust mode. With dropping oil prices and the now long completed pipeline's construction no longer pumping construction cash into the local economy, the town was sinking into a financial recession.

It was January 1979 when a young, second-year trooper, John Adams, reported for third-shift duty at the Fairbanks post.

He was greeted at the door by his sergeant, Tim Cambell, with an emergency. "We have multiple accidents up the Dalton Highway. All we know is there are two trucks in different locations. We think there may be an injury at one, and the CB is saying that both are somewhere close to the Yukon River Bridge, maybe around Pump Station #6. Make sure you check your survival gear before you leave and get your ass moving," said the sergeant.

Cold is a relative term in Alaska. If you live in Anchorage, ten to fifteen degrees below zero is kind of a big deal. North and east of the Alaska Range, that's a walk in the park compared to the fourteen- to sixty-degrees-below-zero temperatures commonly reached in the interior. In this kind of cold, if your skin is left exposed to the elements, you'll be lucky to just lose part of a limb. You may also simply freeze to death.

Like many troopers in the Lower 48, at that time, the Alaskan cruiser of choice was the snappy Plymouth Fury, which sported a big block 440 motor, a four-barrel carburetor, and a Posi-traction rear end. The heavy steel reinforced classic muscle car weighed more than six thousand pounds. It was equipped with wilderness tools, survival gear, and studded tires. During the intense winters in Fairbanks, they were always left running and were almost never turned off except to have the oil changed.

The trooper drove off into the fifty-below winter darkness traversing solid, ice-packed roads as he picked up the Elliot Highway just outside of the Fairbanks city limit. "The road was unusually slick that night. Ice fog was everywhere, and about all I could muster without losing control of the cruiser was twenty-five to thirty-five miles an hour," remarked Adams.

Heading north, the trooper soon lost radio contact with Fairbanks because of the hilly terrain with poor line of site. Back in the late seventies, Citizen's Band (CB) Radios relayed the only communication on the highway. When someone needed help, or truckers reported road conditions, it was all done by CB. Even today, the radio still plays an important role since there is almost no cell service on the Dalton.

As any first responders will tell you, poor information is one of the single greatest factors in restricting their ability to deliver help. People in harm's way are scared, upset, and often not capable of delivering an accurate assessment of their location or circumstance. When you take that scarce information and then pass it between fifteen people before it gets to the responder, you have spotty intel at best.

The Haul Road is a tough, unforgiving driving master. In return, you simply adapt to the intensely steep grades and ice-covered surfaces. This is no ordinary road. There is no cell service or public Internet connection along the Dalton Highway even today. Truckers have affectionately named some of its prominent features, including: The Taps, The Shelf, The Bluffs, Oil Spill Hill, Beaver Slide, Oh Shit Corner, and The Roller Coaster.

In time, you learn to use your low gears, stay off your brakes, and choose your driving lines carefully. Even the best drivers eventually end up in the ditch. And on the Dalton, that ditch could be deadly—the roadbed on flat ground averages a minimum of fifteen feet above the surface with a much wider footprint at the base. Considering the steep inclines and filled-in ravines, it's not uncommon to have a shoulder that falls off at a twenty-plus-degree incline into the black abyss of rock and gravel sometimes more than two hundred feet to the bottom.

With the treacherous road conditions, Adams reached the first accident scene just three miles before the Yukon River Bridge nearly three hours after his departure. "I picked up some CB traffic that indicated the first accident had no injuries, but was restricting traffic southbound and the Dalton was closed at the site. On my approach, I could see the truck lights of a Kenworth tanker on its side, and it was literally taking up the entire roadbed. There was another truck parked on the north side of the downed tanker, yet the scene initially looked calm," recalled Adams.

Once the trooper verified that the driver was okay, he asked the now marooned southbound trucker if he had seen any indication of an accident north of the site. The answer was a firm no. Adams then went to work assessing the scene for his report and planning the procedures with the driver to have the truck removed.

Thankfully, fluids were not leaking from the truck. However, the tank was full of diesel fuel and would have to be pumped dry before the truck could even be moved to the side for traffic to pass, let alone be towed away.

The CB chain rattled with chatter during the early morning hours with traffic passing information from sites north to Coldfoot and south to Fairbanks. A blur of messages were left for the State Troopers, the Alaska Department of Transportation (DOT), a wrecker service, and the company who owned the truck. After an hour and a half, the trooper confirmed a plan was in place to safely remove the fuel and tow the truck away. This event would easily keep the Haul Road closed for the next twelve hours. It was now nearly 3 a.m., with temperatures hovering at fifty-nine below.

"I was frantic to go north, but there was no way to maneuver the cruiser around the wrecked truck. One of the most frustrating aspects of the job is when you realize that you simply may not be able to help someone in need. Today a trooper could use a satellite phone. At the time, I had to depend on the CB chain to clear the accident," said Adams.

Frustrated and worried, the trooper turned the Fury around and slowly headed back toward Fairbanks. The cold was settling in, and he was appreciative of the Plymouth's strong heater turned to high and blowing on his frozen, insulated Chippewa leather boots.

It was only ten miles south, while navigating down a steep, short hill, when Adams—traveling at just twenty miles an hour—started to lose control of the Fury. He was in second gear, near the bottom of a 10 percent short-grade descent, when the 1977 Plymouth sharply fished to the side and started to slide to the passenger side of the road. "I couldn't believe that I was heading for the ditch!" Adams said.

At this moment, he also realized he had unbuckled his seat belt just two miles back when he had reached into the back seat for his parka. He knew that the bottom of the hill featured a classic: steep ravines filled in with bedrock and gravel. It was definitely going to be a long way down before he stopped.

"I would love to tell you that I wasn't that worried, but I knew this could be really, *really* bad," Adams said.

Although he wasn't moving that fast, the Fury's studded tires did nothing to stop it from smoothly slipping to the fringe of the dark abyss, instantly cresting the edge of the roadbed and forcing the sideways car to flip as it left the road. Adams admitted he actually closed his eyes tight and braced himself forcefully into the seat, holding the steering wheel so tight that he thought he might break it.

"I just couldn't believe this was happening and I didn't have a seat belt on. I yelled, 'Ohhhhh F—' and cruiser went off the edge!"

It's not easy to completely destroy six-thousand-plus pounds of Detroit iron, but Adams was well on his way as it rolled, crushing every outside inch of the car. He's not sure how many times it rolled, but judging by the vertical distance he'd fallen, it had to have been at least four times.

"You know, I remember the sound of the glass not just breaking, but actually exploding while I heard the engine revving, probably because I must have hit the gas during the roll," said Adams.

As the cruiser came to a violent upright stop, the trooper was completely disoriented. However, the roof of car was intact . . . sort of.

"I have no idea how long I sat there before I opened my eyes. I don't think I was unconscious, but who knows? I do remember that while my eyes were still closed, I started to systematically move parts of my body. First my foot, then my right leg, then my left, and so on. It was terrorizing to consider opening my eyes, because I was afraid I might be missing a limb and bleeding. I do remember the feeling of intense cold rushing in and the motor still running. So, I decided to slowly open my eyes."

Fighting the disorientation and feeling as though he'd been beaten to pulp in a boxing ring, the trooper gradually cracked his eyes open one at a time.

"I could see tons of steam with only one of the headlights shining. I shut off the engine and looked down to see if my legs were still there, and then looked down at my hands."

Everything seemed okay, but the trooper knew because of adrenaline and the extreme cold, crash victims are often completely numb to life-threatening lacerations or broken limbs. With the engine turned off and the steam now starting to clear, Adams could see something lodged in front of the thoroughly trashed cruiser. His view was better than one would expect because of the lack of windshield. He wasn't sure . . . but it kind of looked like the rear frame of a flatbed tractor-trailer.

"At first I really thought I was seeing things, but then I realized that there was actually a flatbed trailer at rest twenty inches in front of the cruiser!" Adams said.

The trooper started to yell to the driver. Not hearing a response, he decided to climb out of the cruiser. "Getting out was pretty easy considering all the glass was long gone, mostly cracked in small pieces up on the hillside. My parka still had the gloves in the pockets, and it was thankfully resting on the car's floor. I grabbed it, shook the glass off, and quickly climbed out the driver's door."

Adams was, in fact, at the bottom of a 150-foot sloped rock embankment. He started to diligently work his way through tight alders up to the cab of the twisted Kenworth. As he peered back, he realized his Plymouth was completely vacant of intact glass. He kept yelling as he headed toward the tractor trailer. As he clamored closer to the cab, he pondered whether this operator was going be dead, unconscious, or maybe not even there. His mind raced as he surmised how anyone would have not heard the roar of his Plymouth doing summersaults down the hill right behind him.

He took a deep breath as he climbed up on the deck of the bent, disheveled tractor. Silently, he hoped he wasn't going find a man sliced into two pieces or frozen solid. As he peered into the truck, he was relieved to see that no one was in the cab. And, as best he could tell, there was no blood. Based on the description and the lack of snow on the debris, he apprised the rig had only been there a few hours, and he was sure it was the truck he was looking for.

Adams then figured it was time to get out of the ditch. Now cold, he finally put his parka and gloves on and started to climb the rocks up the hill. "I wasn't feeling too great, but it was such a relief to find the missing wrecked trailer with no one stuck inside. I actually was feeling about as good as a man can after rolling a Plymouth four times down a 150 foot embankment."

As the trooper crested the hill, he remembered a sleeping rig was parked five or six miles between him and the wreck in a pull-off. With his Timex watch broken, there was no way to be sure how long he had been down in the ditch. Because he was relatively warm, the assumption was that it had not been very long. But, not knowing, he assessed he had better keep moving to stay warm. He was hopeful his fellow troopers would be looking for him.

At about that time back in Fairbanks, with shift change only an hour away, Sergeant Cambell was troubled. He had neither heard nor received a clear message that Adams was on his way back or had found the second truck. The sergeant did have word that the tanker had been found and the trooper had been on the site. In January, sunrise was really more like twilight and occurred around 11 a.m. It lasted a mere two hours. With temperatures hovering close to fifty-eight below, everyone at the station agreed it was time to find Adams. The day duty Sergeant, Loteria, had arrived early and was apprised of the situation. He immediately agreed with Cambell; it was time to get somebody in the air.

With great concern, Loteria called a Fairbanks Wildlife Trooper who flew one of the agency's Super Cubs and requested he get out of bed to help them. He told the Frog Daug, as they were referred to in those days, that Adams hadn't reported in and that they knew the road conditions were nearly un-drivable. "I really need you to get up there and see if you can find him. It's almost minus sixty, and will get even colder in a few hours."

The pilot said, "I'll be in the air in twenty minutes."

Flying a small plane at night is seriously dangerous business in good conditions over flat land. Add the mountainous terrain of the Alaskan Brooks Range and even the most experienced pilots just simply won't attempt it. The trooper-pilot pulled the plane out of the heated hangar. He headed north, meticulously navigating the shadow of the highway in the darkness.

Meanwhile, it had been a brisk walk for a really sore Adams while trekking back up the Dalton. The two hours of walking gave him time to consider the amazing coincidence of him wrecking his cruiser at the same spot, in exactly the same way, while landing him in front of the missing truck. "It made me feel a little better that the section of road was so nonnegotiable that I wasn't the only guy who couldn't handle it," Adams said.

At about the time Adams was terrorizing the sleeping driver by knocking on the glass in the middle of wilderness, the sound of a Super Cub passed over him. He could hear it turn, and he knew it was looking for him. Adams had the foresight to stand in front of the running lights of the parked semi, which gave him the chance to signal to the pilot on the amazingly low second pass that he was okay. With the plane above the line of site, a radio message came into the Fairbanks station that Adams was found, looked fine, evidently had no cruiser, and provided a mile marker location on the parked semi.

It had turned out the ditched flatbed was driving with a partnered truck. The other driver saw the wreck and helped the operator out of the rig. The stranded driver sustained only minor injuries. As part of a CB chain of messages, the information didn't get back to the troopers for several hours.

Adams chuckled. "The poor guy in the sleeper thought I was a moose kicking at the cab, but he quickly figured out it was human noise and not a threat. Then the sound of the airplane added to the strange and unusual evening the groggy driver was having."

The confused trucker asked if the trooper was okay and asked what Adams wanted him to do. Adams responded, "This heat is so nice. Since you're headed northbound and the road is closed and it's so nasty to the south, let's just stay here. Now that the plane has spotted me, someone will be along in a few hours to pick me up. Hey, you got anything to eat?"

Adams was thrilled to be in the heat and out of the cold. He inhaled one of the trucker's bologna sandwiches, gulped down some coffee, and enjoyed a couple hours of Johnny Cash and Porter Wagner on the 8-track. Two and half-hours later, another trooper's Plymouth Fury pulled up alongside the stationary rig. Adams got out of the truck, thanked the driver, and hopped into the cruiser. At the helm of his ride was Sergeant Loteria, who looked relieved and happy to see the young Trooper.

"So, you've had quite an evening, Adams. And I have to say, it's good to see you. You look far better than I had imagined," said Sergeant Loteria. Adams started to tell the Sergeant about the momentous wrecking of the Fury in addition to discovering the missing truck. "No Shit? You really destroyed the Plymouth? Ah . . . it's the cost of doing business. Let's get you home and then you can take a couple days off."

During the late seventies and early eighties, the troopers at the Fairbanks post were notorious for their once-a-month-ish winter poker games to pass the dark winters. Twenty-five years later, Adams received word that Sergeant Loteria was suffering from terminal cancer. Adams and the former poker group of Troopers quickly traveled to the remote town of Haines for their first poker game in twenty years.

Trooper Sergeant Loteria passed while the group was just two hours away on the ferry. During my interview with Adams, he solemnly stared at the floor and simply said, "Loteria was one of the best men I had ever worked with."

Denali State Park Bear Mauling

Located 100 air miles north of Anchorage, Denali State Park is divided roughly in half for 38 miles by the George Parks Highway, the major road linking Anchorage and Fairbanks. Its 325,240 acres, almost half the size of Rhode Island, includes some of the most visually impactful wilderness in the world. The state park rests between the Talkeetna Mountains to the east and at the foothills of the Alaska Range to the west, offering the closest views of Denali (Mount McKinley) that can be reached by vehicle.

At the south-viewing platform at Mile Marker 135, you are less than 40 miles away from Denali's peak of 20,320 feet. With the turn-off at an elevation of 400 feet above sea level, it is one of the single greatest vertical mountain rises in the world.

To the north and northwest, the state park borders Denali National Park, to the southeast are the Talkeetna Mountains, edging the Susitna basin with numerous wilderness parcels of private and Native Corporation lands. Much of the state park has lightly used wilderness trails that branch off from the Parks Highway. There is only a single campground at Byers Lake and Troublesome Creek. This area attracts hikers from all over the world, and make no mistake—once you're a step or two off the highway, you are in true wilderness.

On July 23, 2011 at approximately 8:40 p.m. a PLB (personal locator beacon) sent an emergency help signal from a location forty miles northeast of the village of Talkeetna in the foothills of the Talkeetna Mountains.

With the Talkeetna Trooper Post shutting down for the evening, Terrence Shanigan was finishing up his paperwork. Meanwhile, first-year Trooper Michael Shelley was on patrol in his cruiser on the Parks Highway.

At 9:30 p.m., Shanigan was notified of the emergency PLB activation and was given a GPS location with an emergency contact phone number. He immediately called the number, reaching a staff member of the National Outdoor Leadership School (NOLS) to ascertain who could be in trouble and what the circumstance may be.

Founded in 1965 by legendary mountaineer Paul Petzoldt, NOLS takes students of all ages on remote wilderness expeditions and teaches them technical outdoor skills, leadership, and environmental ethics.

The school, based in Lander, Wyoming, teaches wilderness survival skills and, during this particular summer, had twenty different groups in Alaska. The teenage students spend three weeks of supervised training in the Bush. On their final week of school, the students are sent out into the wilderness as a group with no instructor and a defined plan to arrive at a specific destination at a set time. The group of seven teenagers ranging in age from sixteen to eighteen were on their solo trip on the southeast side of the Parks Highway in the lower Talkeetna Mountains the evening the PLB was activated.

The school officials assured Shanigan that the students understood to set off the PLB only in a traumatic event when a serious injury or loss of life is possible. They also verified that this particular locating device was nearly impossible to activate by accident. It was determined that the group was backwoods experienced, well trained in survival and first aid, including one participant with WFR or Woofer (Wilderness First Responder) training.

Shanigan immediately contacted Trooper Michael Shelley asking him to meet him at the Talkeetna Post at Mile Marker 99, just off the Parks Highway. While trooper Shelley was en route back to the Post, Shanigan promptly started the procedures to have Helo-1 respond. He also contacted the Joint Base Elmendorf-Richardson outside of Anchorage to request the Air Guard's 210th Rescue Squadron PJ crew to stand by.

A quick series of three-sentence phone calls determined that Helo-1 was on the ground near Fairbanks. The crew had just finished a rescue mission and was already on "overtime" for the pilot, Mel Nading.

About the same time, the Army responded to the Trooper's standby request with challenging news. "Our only available team is at home in bed, and a couple of our guys are out fishing. I'll track them down, but it's going to take a little time," said the Army contact.

The news for Helo-1 was only marginally better. Due to Nading's "overtime" status, it would take approval from the governor to allow the pilot any more flight time.

Shanigan fielded calls back to the school, his commanders, the governor's office, and the military at a feverish pace. Although the weather in Talkeetna was good, reports of fog and rain were surfacing for the area north in the upper Chulitna and Susitna river valleys.

Between calls, Trooper Shelley arrived at the Post and the two officers pored over a map of the area. The two discussed the possible causes for the emergency. It was salmon season and the beacon was activated near a salmon creek. Given that location, they knew water was shallow and not glacial, so it's most likely not a drowning. The cover is thick with alders and small birch. The two looked up and together said "Bear attack!" at the same time.

This information gave Trooper Shelley a guide to collect the gear he needed. He then isolated the right kind of medical kit along with a shotgun with slugs. Understanding that even though it was inevitable that he would be dropped-in by air, he knew there was no way to know how far he would have to walk. Since the terrain could be immensely thick and less than hospitable, he opted to travel as lightly as possible with just one backpack. In the interim, he packed a duffle "Go" bag. He added blankets, rope, food, and additional medical supplies to the list of gear that would ride along in the helicopter; he would hopefully be able to leave the additional gear in the helicopter if the landing allowed.

By now, Nading was cleared for three more hours of airtime by the governor's office and would arrive at the Tesoro parking lot just a few hundred yards from the Post. The pilot radioed into the Post en route saying that he was unable to refuel and would need a truck to meet him at the landing site.

Shanigan got on the phone and called the manager of the Talkeetna Airport, who was at home. Shanigan urgently requested a refuel by truck at the Parks Highway fourteen miles south of town.

Talkeetna medical first responders were now also on notice about the possibility of the attack. They now were on standby to assist in the coming hours. With the Eurocopter refueled and packed with emergency gear, lift off was just past 2:00 a.m. Shanigan stayed behind to continue to serve as the command coordinator.

The flight took less than thirty minutes. There was some twilight, but as the cloud cover increased closer to the GPS coordinates, visibility was less than ideal. During late July, the sunset for this area in Alaska is typically at 11:15 p.m., reaching full darkness at 1:00 a.m. Sunrise begins at 3:30 a.m., with full sunrise at about 5:00 a.m.

Once they reached the coordinates, a first pass showed no signs of activity in the dense creek ravine. Nading raised the altitude to a safe height and donned a pair of night-vision goggles. With the next pass at a slower speed, the pilot spotted a slight flapping that looked like it may have been a tent. With no signs of human activity from the air, the pilot managed to maneuver the helicopter within thirty yards of the coordinates.

Landing in the dark on unfamiliar ground is always a risk. After a thorough, careful ground testing, Trooper Shelley was on the rail. It was determined that the ground would support the weight of the helicopter. It was nearly 2:30 a.m. when Nading shut down the helicopter.

Shelley emerged from the alder thicket ready to encounter a bear. He found three young men, two with deep scalp lacerations. One said, "We're so glad to see you! We were attacked by a grizzly around 8:30 p.m. The guys in the tent are in really bad shape."

As he entered the tent, the trooper found two boys standing and two lying down covered in blood-soaked jackets. Inside the tent, the boys told the Trooper about the injuries.

The two boys on the ground had serious wounds. Although they appeared stable, the injuries were complicated by lung punctures, as well as chest and facial lacerations. Nading came in the tent, and he and Shelley discussed the procedure to remove the group.

Everyone agreed that the two most serious injuries should not go with Nading. Instead, they should be moved in a lying position by stretcher on a medically equipped helicopter. They feared that if the two injured teens were asked to make the walk, or even to sit up, the lung punctures and deep lacerations could reopen.

Nading returned to Helo-1, called on the satellite phone, and notified the station that it was indeed a bear attack. He indicated there were two critically injured boys, and he was requesting additional assistance from the Rescue Squadron PJ crew. He also said he would be returning to Talkeetna with the less injured students. At this juncture, it was 2:45 a.m.

Shelley was particularly impressed with the actions of the students. The first aid rendered to the most severe injuries demonstrated calm, well-trained skill. This included not only finding, but also managing the young man's punctured lung. The dressings were clean, applied with forethought, and were holding effectively.

With the updated phone call, a relieved Shanigan called in the Talkeetna EMS to meet the helicopter. He then delivered a detailed update to the National Guard Rescue Coordination Center (RCC) and the school in Wyoming.

"The students took the appropriate and essential steps to help themselves," said Shelley. "They took measured backcountry medical actions. They wisely chose not to move the most severely injured boy. Instead, the group stripped him of his wet clothes and then pitched a tent over him. To keep his body temperature up, they emptied water bottles, urinated in them, and then applied the water bottles to the boy's armpits while they wrapped him in dry jackets and clothing."

Shelley, who had more than seven years experience as mountain rescue first responder, said that, from a treatment standpoint, there was little left for him to do except to offer calming praise to the group efforts. His role was to try to reduce the emotional trauma they had just experienced.

Meanwhile, Nading moved the four less injured to Helo-1. The bird was airborne at 3:03 a.m. heading back to Talkeetna. He left Shelley, along with the two critically injured students. One of the uninjured teenagers, a sixteen-year-old NOLS EMT-trained student, volunteered to stay behind. They agreed they would wait for the RCC PJ's even though, as of yet, there was no confirmation when they would arrive. Shelley decided that if Nading had a problem, he should keep the satellite phone. "After all, they know where were and what our status was. I knew they would be coming as fast as possible, and calling in would not make it any sooner," said Shelley.

It had been ninety minutes since Trooper Shanigan had heard from Nading. He was relieved when the call came in that Helo-1 was intact and inbound to the Talkeetna airport with survivors. "It was a long ninety minutes," said Shanigan. "I hadn't heard anything. I was starting to fear the worst, like the bear returning, or even a crash."

Within twenty minutes, Helo-1 touched down at the Talkeetna Airport with Trooper Shanigan, and the fire and EMS crews were ready. The boys were quickly loaded on to an ambulance and transported to Mat-Su Regional Hospital seventy miles away in Wasilla. With Nading close to being timed-out, and with just enough air time on his extension to get him home, Shanigan had no intention of sending him back up into the Talkeetna Mountains. As the incident commander, he grounded the pilot and sent him home for rack time.

The EMS crew standing by was less than pleased. They wanted to airlift a paramedic into the area to assist. Shanigan informed the group that based on the information at hand, the rest of the rescue was now in the hands of the RCC. Although Shanigan had not received word of the RCC's departure, he knew it would be soon. Thirty-five minutes later, the trooper was informed the RCC crew was ready to depart Anchorage. They gave Shanigan an ETA that they would be on-site before 6:00 a.m.

Given all of the commotion from the helicopter and activity, there was little doubt that the bear was most likely gone. Armed with a 12-gauge riot shotgun, Shelley did a quick check of the perimeter to find the camp in complete disarray. Clothing and camping gear were strewn and tossed everywhere. A chilling sight, it reminded the trooper just how frightening the experience must have been for the group of students.

While back in the tent with the three boys waiting for the RCC, greater details of the attack emerged.

Evidently, the group was crossing the creek in a line with no idea a bear was so close. It seemed the group neither saw the grizzly, nor was the bear aware of their presence due to the noisy water and wind direction. The student that was attacked first said all he saw was a brown blur and then he was flat on the ground. Despite a resounding yell—"Bear!"—the students were midstream and not able to stand their ground. Then, everyone scattered.

The bear caught the second student immediately after the first. It then chased after the group. The bruin caught two more students, swiping them to the ground. Then the bear returned to the first boy, mauling him again and again, until he remained motionless. Although the group was carrying bear spray, the rate of speed in which the bear attacked left them unable to deploy the deterrent.

The first and last students attacked suffered the worst injuries.

The RCC Jayhawk Helicopter arrived in the daylight, three hours later, at about 5:40 a.m. Without shutting down the engine and while the two pilots remained in their seats, the PJ's, with remarkable efficiency, had the two critically injured students secured in the helicopter in less than twelve minutes. With the non-injured student seated, and after a quick discussion with Shelley, everyone agreed staying at the site was a less than ideal situation. The trooper boarded the Jayhawk and traveled to Providence Hospital in Anchorage 140 air miles to the south.

While the RCC rescue was well on its way, Shanigan determined during one of the discussions with the NOLS School staff members that another group was a few miles away and should be removed from the area. A private Era Helicopter was dispatched to pick up the other group.

Alaska Fish and Game believed that the attack was defensive in nature. Although a cub was not seen, the events that unfolded were consistent behavior of a sow with cubs. Incidents with adult bores, although much more rare, often end in death to the victims.

This bear contact was unique. To date, few documented attacks show bears leaving their victim, or possibly a second, to run after another individual, let alone chasing down two.

The bear was not searched for and is mostly likely still at large at the time of this writing.

Beating the Odds

Living in Alaska on an ice sheet at the ocean's edge is clearly one of the most physically challenging existences on the globe. Despite these formidable circumstances, Native Alaskans have survived with little to no help from the outside world for what some scientists now speculate is more than twenty thousand years.

Shishmaref (pronounced SHISH-muh-reff) is a traditional Inupiat Eskimo village with a populace of 562, according to the 2010 Census. Resting above the Arctic Circle, it is well known for its traditional, subsistence hunting and fishing lifestyle as well as producing fine native ivory carvings displayed all over the world.

It's located on Sarichef Island, part of a long chain of small, uninhabited barrier islands that face the massive Chukchi Sea in the Bering Straits to the west and the protected inland Shishmaref Inlet (bay) to the east side. The village is five miles from the mainland as part of the Nome Borough. The coastal community is surrounded by salt water and is under constant threat of flooding during seasonal high water events. And at only 85 miles from the Russian coast, it is definitely possible to see Russia from any backyard in the village.

Today, many of the barrier islands along the Chukchi Sea are experiencing serious erosion because of rising temperatures. The melting permafrost is unsettling the soil below and making deterioration an extreme challenge. Even tidal barriers have barely slowed the emerging higher seas. The rising seas may, in just a few more decades, completely displace many of these far north villages on the northwestern coast of Alaska.

Like many coastal villages, the primary law enforcement consists of a Village Public Safety Officer or VPSO. The nearest trooper posts are split between Nome to the south, and Kotzebue to the east, and both are roughly an even hundred air miles away.

It was a late October evening in 1996, with winter settling in by creating the season's first heavy ice on the inland bay. The air temperature that night was a steady five below in Shishmaref, with winds gusting to more than forty miles per hour. Visibility was intermittent due to blowing snow.

The ice was believed stable on the bay. Local villagers were starting to use snow machines to travel across the frozen water to hunt on the mainland, five miles on the other side of Shishmaref Inlet.

At 7:00 p.m., Trooper Mike Sears was at home in Nome, on-call, when he received a call about an emergency rescue in Shishmaref. The VPSO had placed a call to let the trooper know that the village was moving ahead with a rescue. A man was stuck in the ice, holding on to his snow machine, with just his head sticking out of the water.

Sears wanted to send an Air National Guard rescue team, however, the weather was deteriorating quickly. High winds were making the blowing snow visually treacherous for a chopper crew. "I'll call the Guard, but you need to be prepared for them not to respond. I'll authorize any kind of payment to the village emergency service team for whatever resources you have. Unfortunately, I can't see the weather breaking enough for the Air Guard until the wind dies down, and that won't be until daylight tomorrow. How long has the man been in the water?" the concerned Trooper asked the VPSO.

The VPSO said he understood the circumstances. He asked the trooper to please deploy the chopper if the weather changed. In an urgent tone, he let him know, "We'll handle it. I'm pretty sure he's been in the water for nearly an hour. I gotta go," and the VPSO hung up the phone.

Sears immediately made calls to the Air National Guard and received confirmation that they, in fact, could not fly until the weather changed.

Since the VPSO understood he would only hear from Sears if there were news of an impending air rescue, he turned to travel logistics.

In a preemptive move, Sears began making arrangements to travel to Shishmaref with an air transport company to pick up the body the next day. Calls were also made to the local hospital and to the coroner's office.

The man in trouble was a village elder named John Sinnok. He was snow machining across the inlet with his twenty-two-year-old son on separate sleds. While running across the bay, the elder father went through the ice. However, with the help of his son, he was able to get out of the water while leaving the sled immersed on the bottom of the inlet. Soaking wet, the father got on the son's sled, turned around, and headed back to the village.

It was only a few minutes after the first accident when the son's sled with the father on the back plunged back through the ice, immersing both men into the icy water. Now, lodged in a much larger hole than the one made by the first sled, the son was separated from his father. He managed to swim to the edge, pulled himself out of what was now an extremely large hole, and climbed up on to the ice. However, he could not reach his father without going back into the water.

The young man's father was conscious and was now holding on to the sunken sled with just his head sticking out of the stingingly frigid water. He told the boy not to get back into the water. He was worried that due to the exertion and the freezing temperatures, the young man wouldn't have the strength to escape the thinning ice shelf a second time and would most likely perish. With the lights of Shishmaref flickering and beckoning in the distance, Sinnok told the boy to abandon him and run back to the village to get help.

Battling five-below temperatures while soaked to the skin, the young man ran over the ice. He followed the snow machine trail for four miles back to the village and put out the call for help.

As soon as the boy was seen in the village, the alarm sounded and resources and help from other village members were instantly set into motion. Within just five minutes, more than one dozen men were revving up snow machines and racing out to the ice hole at high speed.

A short, forty minutes later, Sears's phone rang and the VPSO said, "They got him." A number of thoughts raced through Sears's head. He thought they had recovered the body. He started to say he had already made arrangements for the body to be picked up, and was so sorry for the loss to the village, and hoped the boy was doing okay, but the VPSO said, "No, no, you don't understand. John's at the clinic being treated for exposure. He's going to be okay, and he's in a pretty good mood."

Elated yet completely shocked, Sears could not believe that not only was the man was alive, but also that he seemed relatively okay. This was someone who had spent more than seventy minutes up to his neck in thirty-three-degree water with only his head exposed to an air temperature of five below. Knowing this kind of winter event rarely ends well, Sears had already booked a flight to the village on the first available commercial fight on Baring Air for the next morning. It was the same plane that would have, on the return flight, brought back the body of John Sinnok.

Upon arrival in Shishmaref, Sears noticed a definite joyous feeling among its residents, who were spared from having to plan a funeral for a deceased elder of the community. Sears was met by the VSPO and taken by snow machine to John's home.

There, the man was drinking a hot drink with his son while sitting by the stove in the house. "I just had to meet you sir," said Sears. "I can't imagine the challenge you faced yesterday." Sears also was complimentary to his son. He praised his valiant effort to do as his father asked—not going back into the water and instead getting help so quickly.

Sears really thought the entire experience was even more remarkable when he realized that John Sinnok had no more than

3 percent body fat at most and wasn't close to even five and a half feet tall.

Sears listened closely to Sinnok's remembrance of waiting for his son. "I watched him run away, and I thought that at least I knew he would be alright."

As the night wind blew, it was hard to concentrate on hanging on to a bar on the sled. He knew that if he would let go, he would not have enough strength to pull himself up on the ice. He knew there were currents in the bay from the tides that could easily sweep the weakened man under the ice shelf. He simply had to hold on or die.

All Sinnok could remember that morning was that he could hear the sound of snow machines coming toward him in the distance. And wearily, he wondered if they would be able to find him on the large sheet of ice on the bay. He knew his snow machine tracks would be starting to disappear because of the high winds. Sinnok told the trooper that when he saw the headlights, he must have passed out, because all he remembered was waking up on the transport sled almost in town.

Sears was astounded at the calm tenacity the Eskimo showed in the direst of circumstances. He went on to say, "This was an extraordinary example of this man's will to live. It demonstrated to me just how tough most of the coastal Eskimos are when it comes to survival skills. Don't get me wrong, the polyester insulated snowsuit he had on probably saved his life. It created an insulating barrier for the man to stay conscious. But there is no way to describe just how tough these people are, and what a clear understanding they have of their environment and its perils."

Traditional Inupiat communities base many children's stories on the demons of the cold and water. Whites often misunderstand this folklore and dismiss them as scary, less than soothing tales. Yet, the telling and retelling of these stories for generations helps to ensure young people have decisive knowledge to draw upon in a life-threatening situation.

These people did just fine for thousands of years without anyone's help. They stayed safe, never stole, fed themselves, their families, and their villagers. The Whites are the ones who complicate their culture.

Trooper Sears was well-liked and respected by many of the communities he served. When asked to comment about his time spent in Nome during the eighties, he said, "I learned that the communities of northwest coastal Eskimos are simply the toughest people on the planet. We could learn a lot from them."

Ice Road Moose

With an average moose weighing in at a solid thousand-plus pounds, the animal presents the most dangerous four-legged living obstacle on the Alaskan road network. Collisions are serious for the occupants of the vehicle as these massive ruminants (the largest of the deer family) become walking brick walls on the two-lane blacktops and gravel by-ways of the state.

When you view a moose close up while seated in a car, all you're likely to see are legs. They are so tall that the vehicle strike often hits their ankles, tossing the moose onto the hood and sending it through the windshield, putting the occupant in grave danger.

Winter is when the most collisions occur. A typical moose, weighing in at roughly one thousand pounds can eat up to seventy pounds of food a day. An herbivore, the deep snow limits the animal's access to its primary food source, willow brows. Moose often congregate by the roadsides where they move freely and find plentiful willow that grows on the road's shoulders. They can be drawn to roadways to lick salt used as a snow and ice melt.

It is commonplace for them to become territorial about the open spaces, causing massive car and truck collisions in addition to charging the occasional child at the bus shelter.

It was a cold winter evening in the Northern Susitna Valley when Trooper Terrence Shanigan received a call from a Wildlife Trooper in Palmer eighty miles away. It was after 7 p.m., the temperature was holding at thirty below, and like most mid-winter evenings, it was as dark as sackcloth.

"Can you help me out? We received a report of a moose hit by a large truck and it's lying in the middle of the road north of Trapper Creek. Valentine, the Wildlife Trooper, is off tonight. Can you get up there and get that beast off the highway? And . . . save me from driving more than one hundred miles?" pleaded the duty officer in Palmer.

Shanigan, who was stationed at the Talkeetna post, was already patrolling the Parks Highway and was only about thirty miles away. "No problem, I'm on my way," he said. With the flick of a light switch and siren, Shanigan drove briskly to the scene to get the moose off the road.

Unless you've viewed an adult moose in person, it's difficult to realize just how dangerous such a large animal is to the public's safety when it's splayed across a dark, winding, wilderness road on a cold, winter night. Any driver would have a difficult time seeing the dark brown-and-black moose lying on the black–ice covered highway. Without some advance visual cue, the driver would most certainly be challenged to either maneuver around the moose or to stop quickly on the icy blacktop. Any vehicle colliding with a thousand-pound block of frozen meat five feet thick at sixty-five miles per hour can be deadly—let alone, in the dark in minus thirty weather conditions.

Shanigan understood this was a highly dangerous situation. The only good news was that he had seen only a handful of vehicles on the road because of the weeknight's low, frigid temperatures.

The George Parks Highway, commonly referred to as The Parks, runs from Fairbanks to Palmer, just north of Anchorage. It is 362 miles long and passes through some of the most beautiful and forbidding wilderness in North America. During the winter, temperatures as low as fifty below are commonplace. There is only one gas station open during the day in Cantwell between Trapper Creek and Healy. A 130-mile stretch runs right through the village at Denali National Park; however, during the winter, much of this part of the highway is boarded up and has little to no cell service.

The moose was located near mile marker 147 of the Parks, about twenty miles north of the McKinley Princess Wilderness Lodge at Mile Post 133, which is closed in the winter, almost to Hurricane Gulch.

By the time the trooper reached the massive roadkill, it had been on the pavement for few hours and had bled all over the road. "Slowing to crawl, I looked at what a mess this animal was. Then I started to wonder how I was going to get it off the highway," said the trooper. As Shanigan assessed the situation, he was relieved he hadn't seen any trace of a truck or car. The air temperature now registered forty below. He set out road flares for the oncoming traffic in both directions. He knew moving this beast was not going to be easy and worried the moose was most likely frozen to the blacktop.

"The first thing I did was back the SUV's exhaust over the head of the moose to see if it might loosen the grip of the ice. I tried to pull on the moose's leg and absolutely nothing moved, at all," Shanigan said.

With hot exhaust streaming down on the head of the moose, the trooper removed the eight-pound splitting maul from the back of the patrol SUV. He heaved it up toward his shoulder and went to work on the frozen animal. Time and again, he mounted continual full swings to the ice-locked lower skin with little movement. Just as the trooper was feeling his swing and found his rhythm, an SUV approached the scene with a driver and three passengers.

"I really didn't think much about it. All I was concerned with was that the driver was going less than ten miles an hour and seemed to have control of the vehicle. Past that, I was wondering how many more times I was going to have to hit this thing before I could loosen him up enough to get a tow strap around its neck to pull him off the road," said the Trooper.

As the SUV heading south from Fairbanks inched by, Shanigan never gave it a second thought. How must it have looked from the driver's and passengers' perspectives? There he was, pummeling a dead moose carcass in the middle of the wilderness at more than forty below. He realized later the occupants looked extremely confused and uncomfortable.

As the maul beating steadily continued, he thought that by now the head might be loose enough to separate it from the pavement. Shanigan put his splitting maul down, straddled the moose's neck with his legs, and inserted his gloved fingers in the nostrils of the animal. He started yanking back on its head and neck, which weighed more than one hundred pounds. He was so engaged in the task, he barely took notice of another SUV heading north traveling about as slow as a vehicle could go without being parked. Out of the corner of his eye, he saw four people blatantly staring at him with expressions of absolute horror.

"I was just glad this was only the second vehicle I had seen. Frankly, I was just relieved that they were traveling at a safe speed past the accident site," Shanigan said.

After several more rounds of moose wrestling, the Trooper was able to lift the behemoth's head and get a tow strap around its neck. With a sense of sweaty relief, he gave the SUV a little gas and the studded tires on the SUV broke the moose free from its ice road bondage.

After picking up the area, the trooper realized he couldn't just move the moose to the side of the road because of the extremely narrow and rocky shoulder. This meant he would have to tow the beast to the next pullout near Mile Post 125 so the moose could be dispensed the following day.

So, averaging speeds of ten miles an hour with his flashing lights on, Trooper Shanigan pulled the thousand-pound rock-solid moose, covered in dry, icy blood, more than twenty minutes to the roadside pull off. He found it challenging to maintain control of the vehicle. At times, he had to crawl around turns so he wouldn't lose the SUV to a snow bank.

Only one vehicle passed him while he was heading south. The passengers' gazes moved from the trooper, to the patrol vehicle, to the frozen cargo. "As they passed me, I noted the mortified expressions on their faces. It was as if they were in a reality TV show and someone would jump out and say it was all a joke," said Shanigan.

With the less than tidy moose lying in wait for a roast rescue from a lucky family on the Moose List, he headed back south and stopped in Trapper Creek. The only gas station for more than one hundred miles from the northerly direction, the Trapper Creek Lodge and Motel was open with one woman working the counter.

Shanigan was interested in some soap, water, and a cup of coffee when the Trapper Creek resident greeted him with a blank look of disbelief. "Trooper, I'm so glad you're here. You will never believe this. A group of Outsiders attending some conference in Fairbanks said they saw a trooper beat a moose to death with an axe. Then he wrestled it to the ground and towed it off into the dark! They wanted to know what kind of crazy people live in Alaska when a law enforcement officer could be so uncaring and heartless to a defenseless, wild animal," she said. They then asked how much farther it was to the airport in Anchorage because they couldn't get out of this crazy place soon enough.

Shanigan was so busy with the extraction of the moose, it had never occurred to him that that only SUV he saw was the same one driving by him three times. "The more I thought about it, I came to realize that it must have looked pretty strange. I should have known they weren't Alaskans because no one asked if they could have the moose. You have to wonder about the story they told when they got home," he said with a grin.

The aforementioned Moose List is a salvage program for road-killed moose that started in Alaska in 1978. It's a file the state keeps for locals who will remove and butcher a road-killed moose. Each year, a member from your family can go to a trooper station and fill out an application to be added to the list.

Any Trooper can access the list of area-specific names of individuals. If called, the members must be available night or day and must bring at least three adults to the site to butcher the animal. It is recommended the group bring winching equipment and a trailer.

Troopers are responsible for dealing with moose killed on roadways because the roads are considered state property. Troopers maintain a list of nonprofit and charity organizations to call whenever a moose is killed in a collision with a vehicle. When a collision occurs, the trooper goes down the list. The first caller that answers gets the moose. If you don't answer the phone or fail to respond to the roadkill, you're off the list until next year and you have to apply again.

Moose are rarely wasted in the state. And, the waste-not-want-not charges that can be handed down are the most serious in the wildlife codebook. Troopers provide a valuable service to the community by giving fresh meat to families and groups that otherwise may not have enough to eat for the winter. Many consider it to be the finest table fare in the deer family. Rural Alaskans make an effort to add it to their diet. Road-killed moose are also donated to local nonprofit charities. A number of high schools have classes in carving and butchering moose.

The Story of Amy Sue Patrick

In August 1991, while working out of the Palmer Post in the Mat-Su Valley, investigative Trooper Dallas Massie received a memo. It stated he would be moved to patrol duty and that his backlog cases should be cleared within the next thirty days.

"All good Troopers kept a clear case load—at least that was what our Commander thought at the time. Yet, I just couldn't help myself. I would comb through the files and take cold cases or difficult ones, because I simply loved the investigative work," said Trooper Massie.

With the memo looming and the thirty-day clock ticking, Massie had just closed a commercial burglary case. Burglars had broken into nine local stores and had removed the stores' safes. The trooper found out that a wanted Kansas felon, known to carry a 9mm with a history of assaults, had organized the gang. Massie solved the case and arrested the man the day after he received the memo.

With Massie's thirty days at a close, and with numerous cases solved and closed, he was now back in uniform and on patrol. On his second day on the streets, a young, eighteen-year-old Mormon girl named Amy Sue Patrick was reported missing.

A fellow patrol officer responded to the call. He thought the girl was probably off with her boyfriend and would eventually show up. The report was filed on a Monday when the girl didn't appear for a shift at her job at a local diner in Wasilla. This behavior was completely uncharacteristic for the girl, who had never even been late to work. As Tuesday passed, there was still no sign of the girl, nor had anyone seen her on Wednesday morning.

Sergeant Bill Tandeske called Massie into the Post from patrol. The sergeant said, "This really has me concerned. I want you to put everything aside, grab Tom Clemons (who had replaced Massie in Investigations) and see what you guys can find out."

"What do you want me to do about my patrol assignment?" Massie asked.

Tandeske said, "Forget about it."

Every Trooper should have a mentor. And, in the case of Trooper Massie, it was Bill Tandeske, acting first sergeant at the Palmer Command Post. Tandeske knew that Massie was driven and achieved results. The sergeant thought Massie's patrol assignment from Command was a tremendous waste of an excellent investigator.

Clemons and Massie got right to work. They pulled the file and drove over to the house where the girl had been house-sitting on the west side of Wasilla.

After Massie read the report, he felt a sense of unease. He disagreed with the previous officer's assessment that the girl would just simply turn up. The two investigators secured authorization from the homeowners, an Asian family currently out of town, to enter the home to do a cursory look.

The first odd thing they noticed was the girl's compact car parked in front of the house. The car was the girl's pride and joy. She had worked long and hard to earn the money to pay for it.

Inside the home, they found her purse with her car keys and wallet inside. There was a half-eaten meal on the kitchen table. Upstairs, on the second floor atrium, there was a Thigh Master left lying in front of the TV set. In the bedroom, her work clothes were strewn on the floor along with her panties.

In the bathroom, a towel was thrown on the floor. A packet of birth control pills sat on the counter, and the last pill had been taken on Sunday. When Massie found the pills, the hair on the back of his neck stood up.

The two Troopers silently glanced at each other. They knew the evidence was adding up, and none of it was looking very encouraging. The parents had told the troopers that their daughter was a neat freak. They said she kept a very tidy room without any coaxing from them.

The two investigators quickly returned to the office and reported to Tandeske and the station's lieutenant, John Glass.

"This is bad," said Massie. "Everything we can determine from the existing reports and interviews with her parents and coworkers indicate that Amy Patrick was a diligent, hardworking kid with no history of reckless behavior," he said.

"She called her mother on the phone every day. And," he continued, "she was as reliable as a rock. Everyone speaks highly of her, and we have absolutely no reason to think that she ran off on some fling with a friend."

The sergeant and lieutenant agreed it was time to put a much greater priority on the case. They added an additional investigator, Dave Churchill. Trooper Churchill had been working a case murder in Glennallen to the west. He would return the next morning.

Tandeske looked at Trooper Massie and said, "Get on this. Wear your street clothes when you come back tomorrow. You're off patrol."

The boyfriend was the obvious place to start. And, within an hour, Massie and Clemons tracked him down at his family's home. His alibi was strong, and the young man cooperated and added critical details to the investigation.

The nineteen-year-old said he had spoken to Patrick on the phone on Sunday evening at around 7:00 p.m. While they were on the phone, something strange happened.

"We were talking, and she said, 'Someone's here at the door, I'll be right back.' After twenty minutes there was no answer, and then I just heard the phone hang up. I didn't know if she was upset with me, or if she just had something else to do. But that was the last time I spoke to her," he said.

Massie verified that the young man was at his parents' house all night. All of his movements over the few previous days checked out.

With the boyfriend initially cleared, the investigators turned their attention on the homeowners. The troopers discovered the family's son was in the process of moving back into the house and had been there on Friday. The family also told them that their son had a girlfriend. They provided the troopers with names and contact information. Further research indicated that the son, William Wanna, had a mental history with some behaviors that aroused suspicion.

With just two hours of sleep in the station, Clemons and Massie decided they would locate Wanna's girlfriend. They wanted to contact her first to see what she had to say about her boyfriend.

It was now Thursday afternoon, and the troopers had located the girlfriend in Anchorage. During the interview, she had indicated that Wanna was sexually curious about fetishes. She described the young man engaged in behavior that concerned the troopers.

Massie asked if Wanna had any friends to whom they could talk. She said, "Yes, you should call Kyung Yoon. He's a Korean American and a student at UAA (University of Alaska at Anchorage). He works as a chemistry researcher in a lab in Anchorage."

"I know he was with William when he went to the house on Friday," the girlfriend said. She also let the troopers know that Wanna was a Slope worker. She wasn't sure when he left to go north, but she was sure he was in the Arctic at the time of her interview.

Kyung Yoon lived close by. The two Troopers went directly to his apartment off Old Seward Highway in midtown Anchorage. When the Troopers knocked on his door, the man answered and let in the investigators.

Clemons and Massie sat down with Yoon at 9:00 p.m. Yoon told them Wanna had a lot of girlfriends and a colorful sexual history about which he liked to brag. Yoon commented, "I don't know if he did anything with the girl, but maybe so. He's a pretty kinky guy."

Yoon also admitted Wanna had been to the Wasilla home on Friday and he was with him. Yoon confirmed he saw Patrick for just a moment, and Wanna had spoken with her. The Troopers finished with Yoon at midnight.

Massie noted that Yoon seemed highly socially uncomfortable through numerous comments and questions. Massie felt that Yoon had problems with relationships with women. The young man was excited to hear about the exploits of his friend, and now suspect, William Wanna.

The investigators were beginning to feel that their suspect, Wanna, was looking like "the" guy. They headed back to the Post in Palmer to grab a few hours of sleep.

The following morning, it was confirmed that William Wanna was on the Slope. He had been on a jet flying north on Sunday. It was also confirmed that the plane he was traveling on had been delayed in Fairbanks before heading to its final destination, Deadhorse.

On Saturday morning, the two troopers boarded an Arco jet to Deadhorse. Tandeske was clear about their assignment: "You guys need to break this case. You need to clear this guy or find out if he did it."

Although the Troopers knew that Wanna had a strong alibi, he was the only real lead they had. Once they headed north to follow up and interview him, it would be easy to verify.

Conditions were quickly cooling; however, all the ice had melted from the summer sun. A driver was assigned to the investigators to take them to Kuparuk, miles away, to see William Wanna. They were given an interrogation room and a corporate travel manifest from the plane to check stations on the road to Kuparuk. "It seemed that although he didn't commit the crime, we had to make sure that if knew who did, he was going to tell us," said Massie.

After four hours of interrogations, the two Troopers dismissed Wanna as a direct suspect.

This brought the two men back to square one.

As soon as they were back on the ground back in Anchorage, they headed back to the Post. A few hours after their arrival, the Troopers held a staff meeting. During that meeting, the sergeant inquired about Yoon and his behavior during the interview.

Massie and Clemons agreed that some of the dialogue had been rather strange. Now that time had passed and they really looked at the comments, Yoon had steered the troopers in the direction of his friend, William. "Before we go any further, let's check the phone records and see if that leads us to Yoon," said the sergeant.

The phone records showed that on Sunday night, a call was placed to the Wannas' residence from Yoon's apartment. The call was one minute long. It was about an hour and ten minutes before the time the boyfriend said that Patrick had answered the door. The troopers calculated the travel time from midtown Anchorage to the west side of Wasilla to be about fifty to sixty minutes.

It was now Monday morning. The Troopers had brought back a cooperating Wanna from Kuparuk. They received a warrant to record a conversation between William Wanna and Yoon. When the two were placed together, Yoon quickly smelled the trap and gave no information.

With the investigation now clearly focused on Yoon, Massie and Clemons went after every detail they could obtain about Yoon and his habits. Yoon was a high-achieving chemistry student at UAA. The man was smart, but lonely. He was despondent to anyone except his family members and Wanna.

The Troopers also ascertained the suspect was unlike his brother, who lived an active, well-socialized American lifestyle as a Korean. Even though Kyung Yoon was born in America, he had few relationships with Koreans or many Americans. He seemed left in an abyss between the two cultures. Instead, he thrived in his studies and in fantasy.

As the week continued, Massie and Clemons searched through a number of trash bins multiple times. Between the two of them, they made nearly one thousand phone calls. They were approaching the two-week mark with very little evidence with which to move ahead.

On Saturday, Dave Clemons said, "Let's talk to him again. What do we have to lose?" Massie agreed. Instead of bringing him into the office, the two Troopers decided to visit him at work, a chemistry lab in Anchorage.

Their joint goal was to fill in the gaps about his personal life. They wanted to keep the interview at a noncustodial level. This allowed the troopers the freedom not to arrest the suspect, unless he confessed. The troopers made it clear that Yoon was not under arrest and could leave at any time.

When the interview started, Yoon was cooperative and felt somewhat empowered. Through experience, Massie and Clemons understood the need to garner personal information about the suspect. Their ability to communicate with the suspect in a trusting manner would be directly linked to their keen skills to gather this information.

The two men were experienced in this kind of interrogation technique. If the interviewer could be nonjudgmental and personal, they often found violent criminals wanted to disclose their deeds out of guilt. Suspects often viewed it as a form of redemption.

Through their conversation, they found out that Yoon was obsessed with playing the video game, *Dungeons and Dragons*. He had a deep-seated interest in fantasy culture. He painted intricate fantasy figurines and liked to frequent a video arcade in Anchorage. Once there, he played only a few, specific video games. His favorite movie was *Star Wars*.

The troopers directly asked Yoon about his alibi. He said that on Sunday evening at 6:00 p.m., he was at an arcade playing a video game. In great detail, he talked about the game, his score, and other people who were in the arcade at the time.

Afterward, he went home to watch television. Massie just happened to know what was on network television that evening. Massie asked, "What did you watch?" When Yoon gave the answer, the trooper knew immediately it was wrong.

Massie responded with, "Now Kyung, you know that program wasn't on that night."Yoon immediately felt uncomfortable. His body language changed and shifted. He had increased difficulty keeping eye contact with the two investigators.

Massie took one gentle step further. With a large sigh, he shook his head from side to side and said in near whispered tone, "You know you weren't at the arcade on Sunday night."

Both men started to step up the pace. Together, they took turns and became more demanding and accusatory.

Clemons started first, saying, "We know it was you! We know you called the house an hour before she was abducted! It has to be you!"

Yoon looked at the table.

Massie had used the technique of having suspects describe their dreams to find revealing evidence. He had found it was a way for the person to tell you when they did something horrific, but they couldn't face the truth or didn't want the investigators to hate them for it.

"Kyung . . . close your eyes and tell me about your dreams, tell me what you see," coaxed Massie.

Sensing Massie's direction, Clemons backed off and let Massie continue.

Without hesitation, Yoon closed his eyes, took a deep breath, and said with a chilling calm, "I pull up to the house and knock on the door. She answers and lets me in. I cover her mouth with an ether rag and she passes out. I walk through and check the house. I find the phone is off the receiver, and I hang it up. Then I load her into the car and I drive toward Anchorage."

He continued that he passed through a construction zone on the Glenn Highway and pulled off at Pilot Road. Massie asked him, "How far did you go?"

Yoon responded with his eyes closed. "One half mile."

"What did you do?" asked Massie.

With his eyes still closed, he responded in an icy tone, "I snapped her neck, then I dumped her on the side of the road and covered her over with brush."

Yoon opened his eyes and sat calmly in the chair.

The two Troopers were stunned. They now had a confession, but they still didn't have any evidence. Massie decided to walk down the path of Yoon's favorite movie, *Star Wars*.

Not wanting to lose the momentum, Massie asked, "You went over to the Dark Side didn't you? It's a lot like Darth Vader, isn't it?" He continued, "Darth Vader found peace. Tell us the rest."

Yoon solemnly nodded yes. With his eyes open, he filled in some of the details, including the moment he snapped Patrick's neck.

Based on his confession, the two Troopers would need to take Yoon's vehicle. But they decided not to arrest him, hoping he would show them the body.

Massie asked Yoon, "Will you show us where she is right now?"

Yoon said, "Yes. Can I go to my locker and put my stuff away?"

Knowing that he couldn't leave the school without passing by two officers, they let him go to the locker.

While Yoon was at the locker, a call was placed to CID down the street. They would impound the car while they waited for a warrant to send it for a thorough forensic search.

The three men quietly walked to the trooper's unmarked cruiser in the parking lot. They headed to Pilot Road just north of Eagle River next to the Glenn Highway. The trip took about twenty minutes. Yoon rode in the front seat with Clemons and Massie sat in the back behind the suspect.

Pilot Road sits within a few hundred yards of the four lanes of the Glenn Highway. The road dead-ends with a turnaround. In September, there would still be thick, heavy vegetation on the side of the road from the long growing days of near twenty-four-hour light in the summer. It's also an area black and grizzly bears frequent, and the Troopers were concerned there may not even be a body to recover.

They arrived at the half-mile point on the road and stopped the car. The two Troopers saw no sign of a brush pile or anything that looked like what Yoon described. Getting agitated, Massie said, "What's going on? We need to find this body! We owe it to her family!"

Clemons said evenly, "Okay, let's start this over again."

While they sat in the car, the two troopers turned on their tape recorders and went through the events of the previous Sunday night.

At first, they heard the same, repeated information. However, when they got to the part where he snapped Patrick's neck, Yoon added, "I thought it was blood that came out of her mouth, but it was saliva and then her eyes started to flutter. Then I took her out of the car and I put her over there." He pointed to the side of the road. "Then I drove back to Midtown. I went home, got some garbage bags, and returned. I put her in the bags and covered her up. Then I went home again."

Massie followed up and asked, "Okay, you left the body here, then what?"

Yoon replied, "Well, I have class in the morning. So I went to UAA, attended my class, drove back to Eagle River, picked up her body, drove across the highway to the Anchorage City Refuse Station, and dumped the bagged body in the dumpster."

Massie and Clemons were flabbergasted. They had a taped confession with no collaborating evidence. They now wanted to make sure they followed protocol and didn't make a misstep, so they called the district attorney's office in Palmer.

The Dodge was equipped with one of the early bag cell phones. They immediately placed the call. In front of the suspect, the troopers explained the circumstance and asked for the DA to share the prudent next steps.

The DA replied, "I'll tell you what you do with this guy. Take that son-of-a-bitch to the CID headquarters, get the confession again, arrest his ass, and advise him of his Miranda rights."

Massie said okay, and the three were on their way back to Anchorage. Yoon was still cooperative. Although he did become agitated in the interrogation room during the videotaping, the

Troopers again got the same confession, chapter and verse, on tape for the third time.

Yoon was placed under arrest. He was read his rights and Clemons searched him. Massie and Clemons discussed it, and they both decided that they would take Yoon to Palmer.

They stopped at a Quick Shop to get some food for the suspect and headed north up the Glenn Highway. Just past Eagle River, they encountered an extremely erratically driven Chevy Blazer. The operator was clearly intoxicated and a danger to society.

Massie looked over at Clemons and said, "We have to pull this guy over; he's going to kill someone."

Clemons turned on the lights and pulled the SUV over. There were two men in the car. Both doors of the SUV flew open. Massie had to then assist Clemons. Meanwhile, Yoon was handcuffed and secure in the back seat of the cruiser.

Massie left the car for about a minute to help Clemons cuff the intoxicated driver. He made it clear to the Chevy's passenger that he needed to remain in the truck.

With the drunk driver in restraints and sitting on the ground outside of the truck, Massie called Anchorage PD for a car to finish the DWI.

Within ten minutes, the two Troopers were back on the road. By the time they arrived at the Trooper Post in Palmer, it was 1:30 a.m.

Yoon, who had been relatively cooperative, started to get restless and agitated. The men then steadily walked the suspect into the Sally Port for processing at the Mat-Su Pre-Trial facility next door.

The first comment from Massie to the officer at the jail was, "Put this guy on suicide watch. Really, I'm not kidding. Watch him carefully." The receiving officer said he understood, and Yoon was escorted inside to be stripped searched and processed on a murder charge.

Because of Massie's request to watch the suspect, the receiving corrections officers opted to keep Yoon in a secure room where they could easily check on the prisoner.

The prisoner was eventually strip searched later, given prison-issue clothing, and put in a holding cell for arraignment the next morning.

Kyung Yoon was brought into court in the morning.

He held up his hand. On it, he had written, "I lied. It wasn't Ether, it was Chloroform." Within just a few minutes, Yoon collapsed in the court room. He lost control of his bowels and went into a state of shock.

Massie was in the office early that morning. Around 9:00 a.m. an investigator ran by him. He headed out to the parking area and looked through the investigator's car, where he found a small, empty vial.

Yoon was taken by ambulance to a hospital in Anchorage. There, they found high amounts of arsenic in his system, and his organs were in full shutdown. He died later in the day.

Once Yoon confessed the first time, he thought the officers would let him go home where he would commit suicide. When Yoon went back to his locker at his office, he secured a strategically hidden small vial of Arsenious Oxide—an extremely pure poison chemical cocktail. He had hidden the vial in his sock around his shoe so it wouldn't be detected during a weapons search.

While in the car during the DWI stop, he evidently ingested a dose and poured the balance of the poison in his sock. This gave him enough time to take another dose while he was waiting in the corrections room.

The Troopers were all distressed. Certainly, Clemons and Massie had no love lost for Yoon, but they hadn't wanted Yoon to die. Massie, for one, wanted him to suffer for his vicious crime for the rest of his life in jail.

Moreover, Massie and Clemons had numerous unresolved concerns. The greatest of which was locating the young woman's body for her grieving family to have a proper burial.

Trooper Tom Clemons spent three exhausting weeks searching for the body at the refuse station. He was joined by a group of trooper volunteers, including cadets from the Academy and

Anchorage City employees. Together, they searched through the garbage for nearly sixteen hours a day.

Video tape taken from the site showed Kyung Yoon's car had been at the station on the morning he stated. The Refuse Manager informed the troopers that a dead horse and elephant dung were dumped at close to the same time that day.

After three weeks of sifting through untold amounts of refuge, part of the horse was found. Anchorage Refuse employees offered to stay and work for free to find the body.

Two long days later, the body of Amy Sue Patrick was found. She was in extreme stages of decomposition, offering little forensic evidence. The Patrick family buried their eighteen-year-old daughter, Amy Sue, on October 26, 1991.

Since the suicide of Kyung Yoon had taken place while in custody, the Asian community in Anchorage was outraged. Despite the taped confessions, many groups banded together in protest. They felt the Troopers had overstated their authority, and, at the very least, they had violated Yoon's civil rights.

The FBI completed an investigation and released a statement on November 15, 1991. They found that the Alaska State Troopers and Corrections officials did not violate the civil rights of Kyung Yoon.

After internal investigations were conducted, Massie and Clemons were cleared of any wrongdoing. They were issued a reprimand for not completing a more efficient search.

Both men continued with the troopers. Dave Churchill moved from investigations to the Wildlife Troopers. He died of a heart attack while on duty on September 16, 1998. He was checking on a hunting party on the side of a mountain on the Kenai Peninsula.

Massie continued his work in criminal investigations. He solved several murders and served his last Post in Talkeetna. He later retired from the troopers, and then became the Chief of Police in Nome.

Bear Spray Pranks

Jutting from the southern coast of Alaska, the Kenai Peninsula rests 150 miles southwest from the Chugach Mountains in Anchorage. This massive expanse reaches east to the Gulf of Alaska in Prince William Sound and borders the Cook Inlet to the west. As a borough, the equivalent of a county in the Lower 48, it encompasses 25,600 square miles. The landmass of the borough boundaries—15,700 square miles—is equal to the size of Massachusetts and New Jersey combined. The larger towns of the Kenai include Homer, Soldotna, and Seward. Considered relatively populous by Alaskan standards, it has nearly 57,000 residents as of the 2010 census.

Soldotna is located an hour and half north of coastal Homer and three hours southwest of Anchorage. It's a town with more retail services than most Alaskan communities and is at the center of the sport fishing industry's most popular salmon river, the Kenai.

In many respects, duty as a trooper post in Alaska can be unremarkably like many other states' trooper or metro police stations, except few Lower 48 stations keep bear spray on hand.

It was 1995 and Trooper John Adams was now approaching retirement. He had landed a comfortable assignment, stationed in Soldotna, the borough's seat, working the courthouse. Nearing his twenty-five-year mark as a trooper, he had served all over the state from native villages like Ninilchik, to the cold, interior in Fairbanks during the seventies and eighties.

This particular day, he headed to the coastal town of Kenai just thirty miles away to deliver paperwork from the courthouse.

The Kenai police station was staffed with administrative support personnel. In addition, within its several thousand square feet, it shared space with the fire department. Like most stations, there was a temporary holding facility, a large garage, and one of the larger conference rooms on the peninsula. Numerous public service personnel used this room for general meetings and presentations.

Adams was out early that morning, transferring paperwork from the courthouse to other municipalities in the borough, when he dropped by the Kenai police station. The first shift was getting started, and he was hanging out at one of the Kenai officer's cubicles. With two cops looking for a diversion instead of processing court paperwork, the subject turned to bears and the merits of bear spray. A debate ensued and a few contentious questions were raised. First, what was it really like to be sprayed with bear spray? And second, how was it different as compared to the small canisters of mace that most police departments carried? With everyone jacked up on multiple cups of coffee, this conversation lead to the Trooper challenging the Kenai police department as to whether they had the balls to experience the spray first hand. It was one of those trooper-double-dog-dare-you moments.

Bear spray, or Counter Assault Bear Deterrent Spray, is a seven- to nine-ounce preventative designed to safeguard humans during an aggressive or attacking bear confrontation without harming the bear. The spray uses a red pepper base that shoots a powerful, direct stream from twelve to thirty feet and empties in approximately seven seconds. Bears that come in contact with the spray have a history of immediately retreating, leaving the human safe. Compared to most small canisters of mace, bear spray cans are often ten to twenty times larger, displace a far greater stream, and also leave more of the ingredients hanging in the air. The spray is not without controversy among resident Alaskans who generally opt to carry large caliber handguns as bear deterrents. One of the most common accidents of misuse is discharging it into the wind; the contents then reverse direction, disabling the person using the can.

During many departments' training across the country, most police officers that carry stun guns as a deterrent to their use of force are actually stunned or tazed by the weapons so the officer understands the parameters and safe use of the gun. The use of pepper spray can be the same, with training exercises that include a firsthand experience so the officer has a personal understanding of the potentially unpleasant consequences.

With the bear spray discussion peaking in volume from the visiting state trooper and the Kenai officer, the station's Lieutenant Doyle overheard the discussion and asked what the two were talking about. It didn't take long before Adams asked the lieutenant if he had ever been sprayed, even with mace, and whether he was man enough to take it in the face for the Kenai team. The lieutenant gave a resounding expletive and added, "No, are you kidding? I'm not doing that." More bantering ensued and it wasn't long before the senior officer said he had enough of this waste of time. He told the trooper to get the hell back to the courthouse and his officer to get back to work.

Adams felt particularly mischievous that day and decided to prank the lieutenant after he left his office. Adams sneaked into the office and thoroughly sprayed the desk and paperwork and left a slight, hanging cloud of the irritant in the air. As Adams exited the lieutenant's inhospitable domicile, he turned the hall corner and literally bumped into his station captain. After a hurried greeting to his direct and immediate boss, Adams saw the chief of police of Homer walking up the same hall.

He realized that this was the day of the borough's monthly Chiefs of Police meeting and every high-ranking officer on the Peninsula was arriving at the station. The monthly meetings were held to keep an open dialogue between the departments and to review case files so the different departments knew what each group was working on. The meetings were serious, productive, but always friendly, helping to close cases that may not otherwise have been solved.

As the captain turned down the opposite hallway to go into the bathroom, Adams started to hear seriously loud exclamations of "What the f—ck!" exploding from the other side of the door. The spray's lingering effects on the lieutenant's eyes, throat, and nose was a little more than the trooper had planned on.

Like a jackrabbit, Adams grabbed his subpoena file and his jacket and headed to his cruiser in the parking lot as fast as humanly possible without looking like he was in trouble. He passed two Kenai officers who asked him what was going on with the lieutenant. He simply and tersely responded, "I'm due at the courthouse! Gotta go!"

The trooper jumped into his cruiser, threw it into drive, and left the station as fast he could without squealing the tires. While Adams was heading down the road, what he hadn't thought about was the location of the lieutenant's office. It was directly across the hall from the conference room where the chiefs were meeting.

After Adams left, the lieutenant calmed down when he realized every one of his potential future bosses was in the building. Given the illustrious audience, he knew he needed to temper his reactions. Without so much as a thought to what could happen, the officer threw his window wide open and left the door of his office agape to air out the irritant. Clearly frustrated, he marched directly to the bathroom to immerse his face in a sink filled with water.

Just moments before the lieutenant headed for bathroom, the conference room across the hall was now full of non-pranking, unsuspecting brass.

After the lieutenant soaked his face in the bathroom, he figured it was time to step outside the building to catch some fresh air.

About this time, Adams who was like a kid driving around the neighborhood to avoid the high school principal, just had this nagging feeling he needed to pass by the front of the station. When he drove past the entrance to the Kenai station, he witnessed every high-ranking officer of the troopers and neighboring police departments coughing, holding their eyes, and using language that would be not be acceptable at church. Adams said, "They just looked so miserable. I could see one of the Chiefs dripping snot almost to the ground from across the parking lot. I drove by as covertly as possible and I'm pretty sure no one saw me."

When the lieutenant had opened his doors and windows before heading to the bathroom to rinse off, the bear spray had quickly migrated across the hall through the wide open door into the conference room, antagonizing every man at the table. It only took a couple of minutes to send them all outside, where the lieutenant, already afflicted, stood in complete misery.

In less than ten minutes, Adams received a message from dispatch that he needed to report to his captain's office at the Soldotna Trooper Station at 7:00 a.m. sharp the next morning.

Adams now had the notorious reputation of pulling off one of the most brazen pranks in Peninsula Law Enforcement history. Although he generally found cautious respect, he garnered little sympathy from his fellow troopers. The comments ranged from, "Man, that was hysterical" to "I'm glad I didn't do it." Perhaps the one comment he heard the most was, "Aren't you, like, just two years away from retirement?"

The next morning's walk of shame to the captain's office rested heavily on the trooper. He was greeted with a stern sit-down and was handed a piece of paper from a man who still exhibited reds eyes and puffy cheeks. The captain grunted, "Read it and sign it." The trooper read the reprimand from a subservient position in the chair. It really didn't sound as bad as he thought. He signed it, and with just two fingers, he gingerly slid it on the captain's desk.

Adams quietly asked, "Is that all?"

The Captain roared back loud enough for the whole station to hear, "It will be as long as you never do it again! You even think about a stunt like that, and you'll be lucky to get a job on winter crab boat out of Homer, without your pension!"

It turned out the captain was really looking out for the trooper. A few days later, during a procedures meeting at the courthouse, the captain leaned over and said, "Now that your reprimand is out of the way, if the other officers file a complaint of conduct, I'll be able to say you've been reprimanded, it's in your trooper's file, and the issue is closed. This will go away and you know . . . just between the two of us, it was pretty funny."

The Captain never brought up the issue again. From that moment forward, when Adams would run into a Kenai cop, they would often affectionately refer to him as "Pepper."

The Boys from New Jersey, or Home Alone in Skwentna

On April 28, 2010, at 8:30 a.m. a lodge owner called the Talkeetna Trooper Post from the remote town of Skwentna. He reported multiple break-ins in the area, with suspicious activity seen firsthand by the resident. In addition, the sounds of intermittent gunfire were reported in the area.

Skwentna lies on the south back of the Skwentna River at its junction with Eight Mile Creek, a seventy-mile flight from Anchorage. This isolated village is a checkpoint on the annual Iditarod Trail Sled Dog Race from Anchorage to Nome each March in South Central Alaska, as well as a gas stop for the Iron Dog Snowmobile Race in February.

It's located at the confluence of large glacial rivers, the Yentna and Skwentna, with several other smaller streams adjoining upstream, like Lake Creek and Fish Lakes Creek. It has a registered year round population of thirty-seven as of the 2010 census and is known for its excellent salmon fishing and fall moose hunting. The area has more than two hundred remote cabins with some considered austere, but many offering near or surpassing suburban creature comforts that can sell in the multiple six-figure range. The structures are hand built by their owners hauling building materials either up the river by jet boat in the summer, or freight sledding with snow machines or contracted snow cats in the winter. There is an active Roadhouse and a few lodges that operate year round with moderate winter snow machine traffic.

Considered to be the start of the Cook Inlet Delta below the Alaska Range, its large, turbid glacial rivers have carved reasonably flat topography with massively rising elevations to the north and west. Skwentna is the first check point on the Iditarod on the way to Rainy Pass in the Alaska Range, with the "official" race starting just thirty miles away in Willow next to the Parks Highway. Although an outsider (someone from the Lower 48) would consider the Skwentna and the Yentna river valley remarkably inaccessible, its residents would hardly consider it the wilderness. To them, it's more like . . . the edge of the wilderness.

When the area was homesteaded in the seventies, and before the construction of the Parks Highway, summer residents ran small outboard Jon Boats down the Yentna to the connecting Susitna River south to its mouth at Cook Inlet. To buy supplies in Anchorage, twenty miles away, they would often wait twelve hours for the tide to come in to cross one of the most treacherous tidal bays. The journey would often take up to two days in each direction. You would find the permanent residents in Skwentna capable, protective, and experienced in dealing with unwanted visitors.

The acting supervisor of the Talkeetna Station knew Trooper Terrence Shanigan grew up fishing and later guiding in the Skwentna region. He asked him to accompany investigative Trooper Andy Adams to Skwentna as quickly as possible.

The supervisor told the pair that a resident had reported finding extensive damage to multiple cabins including bullet holes shot from inside the buildings, broken and left open windows and doors, along with stranded ATVs and snow machines. That morning, the caller entered one of the vandalized structures and flushed a barefooted man out the second-story window. The intruder landed in the snow and ran off through the woods.

The state of the rotten ice combined with the dangerous river conditions would make it impossible to attempt snow machine travel into the area. And there was still too much ice on the river to consider jet boat travel. A request was put in for the department's helicopter, Helo-1, from Anchorage.

The turbine-powered, Eurocopter AS350 helicopter piloted by the late Mel Nading sat down at the Tesoro truck stop at the Talkeetna Spur and Parks Highway. It picked up Troopers Shanigan and Adams at around 11:00 a.m. From Talkeetna, they were in Skwentna in just twenty minutes, landing in front of the Northwoods Lodge at Fish Lakes Creek. In addition to their sidearms, both troopers had AR-15 patrol rifles and were wearing protective chest armor.

With Helo-1 parked on the beach in front of the lodge, the two troopers were ferried across the creek by the lodge owner using a small Jon Boat. The lodge owner and another resident reminded the two troopers that he had heard random gunfire fast enough to come from semi-automatic guns. With the potential risk high, the troopers asked the residents to stay at the lodge and they would get back to them soon.

With the sun shining and the temperature close to sixty degrees, the troopers found the walking conditions wet and slushy as they post-holed with every step in the soft, two feet of spring snow. The troopers quickly located tracks in the snow traversing up a hill to one of the vandalized cabins.

This particularly large 1,400-square-foot cabin had all the amenities of a home, including flat screen TVs, full bathrooms, a large kitchen, and even a phone. "This was a really nice cabin, and it was an absolute wreck," said Shanigan. The floor was covered in muddy boot tracks, there were broken CDs and DVDs scattered everywhere. Shell casings littered the floor, and most of the damage to the flat screen TVs was from gunfire. A fast search also turned up empty gun cases and open ammo boxes. It was apparent the suspects were collecting firearms from the looks of this cabin break-in.

Walking wasn't easy, and the troopers did their best to move quickly. They tracked the footprints and cleared each cabin systematically. Tension was high. They knew their entrance by helicopter would have never gone unnoticed by anyone close by. The two troopers tactically approached each building and shed as they entered the structures with precision. Each vandalized building had significant damage similar to the first. The two troopers bagged evidence and shot hundreds of digital photos. In most of the cabins, evidence included spent shell casings mixed with cigarette butts from both Marlboro and Newport cigarettes.

Following the tracks led the now-tired and overheated troopers to the edge of a medium-sized stream only half covered in ice. They could see footprints in the fresh snow. Whoever crossed it went into the water and came out the other side. It was time to call Nading in Helo-1 and have him pick up the two officers and to take them across the river.

Nading brought the chopper over, picked up the two troopers, and ferried them over to another cabin with tracks outside. Nading was careful to land the troopers just inches above the snow. He suspected the melting base would not support the Eurocopter.

While closing in on the fifth cabin check, the officers found even more shell-spent casings, finished cigarettes, and a glove. Inside, the vandals had stacked boxes and had climbed them to get to higher cabinets. In turn, this left the troopers some of the best tracks of the day for digital photo evidence.

With another pick up from Nading, the crew flew a circular pattern while they conducted an inventory of footprints and cabins that looked damaged. Watching the ground intently, the troopers tried to figure out which cabin the vandals could be holed up in. From the air, they continued to source several miles of winding trails. Everyone was confident that the barefooted man seen jumping out the second-story window at 7 a.m. couldn't be far.

Given the weather conditions, there was no way anyone could leave the general area without a plane landing at the strip near the lodge or a helicopter.

"They had to be close by, and it wasn't like they didn't know we were there," said Shanigan. The two troopers and the pilot decided to stay in the air to select the most likely cabins. The plan was for the helicopter to take a covered position, sound a siren, and announce the presence of troopers with instructions for the intruders to leave the cabin.

However, the vandals held tight and were not discovered. It was getting close to five in the evening, and the three troopers agreed to fly back to the Station in Talkeetna and debrief. They made a quick stop back at the Lodge with instructions for the residents to stay away from the suspected danger zone and report any gunfire back to the station. If the situation worsened, they would fly back quickly.

On the return flight, Shanigan asked Mel to stop at Lake Creek to check in on an old fishing guide that may have some information. As the Helo-1 slowly descended in front the old-timer's cabin, the jet wash was strong enough to blow over the man's Jon Boat that he was readying for fishing season.

As classic Alaskan bushmen go, Willie the fishing guide was ready for reality television. The older man stood about five feet tall, weighed less than ninety pounds, and had a long beard. He also lacked dental implants for his mostly missing teeth. As a fishing guide on lower Lake Creek drainage, he was famous for ringing a cowbell every time one of his customers caught a fish.

Willie seemed glad to see the troopers and wasn't overly worried about his dislodged boat. As soon as Shanigan got on the ground and cleared the Helo, Willie said, "There's been crazy sh— going on across the river. I've heard a ton of gunfire, and my dog has been missing for three days!" said the old timer. He added, "I think the son-of-bitches killed him!"

Shanigan made it clear that Willie needed to stay out of the area down river and told him the troopers would be back soon. The Alaskan agreed, and they headed northeast. They crossed the even larger Susitna River into Talkeetna. While Shanigan and Adams were getting a workout in the snow and mud, many part-time summer residents received calls that cabins were broken into and the troopers were on the ground investigating. The buzz of the Skwentna news was humming, even in Anchorage, where most of the seasonal residents lived.

One of the calls that came into the station was from a Skwentna cabin resident saying that a guy named Buzz lived in Anchorage and had rented his cabin to a couple of New Jersey college students about two weeks ago.

Shanigan was able to reach Buzz before he signed out that evening by phone. Buzz was cooperative. He told the trooper that a friend at Sportsman's Warehouse in Wasilla told him two guys were looking for an off-the-grid cabin to stay in for a year or more. He ended up renting the two his cabin for a hefty $1,500 a month. The renters agreed to complete some work on the structure in addition to the rent. They could stay in the building until early summer when Buzz's family would show up in mid-June for King salmon season.

The Jersey boys agreed and asked what gear they should bring. Buzz told them, food, sleeping gear, batteries, and so on. The extensive list of off-grid gear had the two young men dropping more than $5,000 for everything from jerky to batteries to plenty of ammo at the Sportsman's Warehouse. With a referral from Buzz, they contacted Rust's Flying Service in Anchorage to transport them to Skwentna by ski plane. Buzz was in tow to show them how to use the cabin and to assign a punch list of repair duties.

Buzz told the trooper that the group flew out on the last day the company would ski fly from Lake Hood in Anchorage. With all the gear the Jersey boys had purchased, a second cargo flight was required. The ice was strong enough in Skwentna for the plane to land on the frozen water right in front of the cabin. Buzz returned to Anchorage on the second flight, leaving the Jersey boys home alone in their new and remote cabin. Buzz said they paid cash for the gear, flight, and rent, which probably totaled close to $10,000.

During the phone interview, the trooper also learned the Jersey boys had parked a van at Lake Hood where Buzz kept a floatplane stored on shore for the winter. While Adams and the Talkeetna station checked more information the following day, Shanigan used what was to be his scheduled day off—which had included a trip to Anchorage a hundred miles south—to interview the flying service that hauled the men to Skwentna and to look for the van at Lake Hood. After talking to a manager at Rust's, the trooper found Buzz's story to be accurate. He then followed up on the description of the cabin owner's plane, which should have been located a half mile away on the other side of the lake. When the trooper located the correct plane tail number, he found the van.

Lake Hood rests in metro Anchorage, next to the Ted Stevens International Airport. It's a state-owned seaplane base located three nautical miles from the central business district. One of the world's largest and busiest seaplane bases, Lake Hood handles an average of 190 flights per day. Nearly 1,000 small and large floatplanes owned by a mix of outfitting services and private individuals are docked at the lake. During the winter, many of the planes are fitted with skis for wilderness access. They take off and land on the lake until breakup—three to six weeks in which conditions throughout the state become too dangerous to fly. Once the ice is gone, floatplanes fly the skies of southeast Alaska, ready for the summer season. A private dock on the lake has a ten-year waiting list.

The blue and white 1980s Ford van rested just where Buzz said it would be, next to his plane on the small lot. The trooper walked silently around the van. As he peered through the window, he found Marlboro and Newport cigarettes in plain view on the dash. A check of the new Alaska plate revealed the van was purchased roughly ten days prior by a Jeff Indellicati. The name didn't show up in the Alaska criminal system. Since the van had just been purchased, there was not enough additional information to run the name on the national database.

He updated the Talkeetna staff by phone and was at the post early the next day.

After a few more calls, the troopers determined the van was illegally parked. Evidence was beginning to mount. Aside from the cigarettes and Buzz's comments, the boot prints at the van matched the ones on the box in the ransacked cabin. There was enough evidence for the trooper to obtain a warrant. The truck was seized and towed to the headquarters in Palmer, forty miles north of Anchorage.

Evidently the presence of the trooper's helicopter earlier in the day did nothing to deter the Jersey Boys because gunfire remained a constant throughout the evening of April 29. This forced the Talkeetna post staff to formulate a plan to go in and stabilize the area.

Shanigan enlisted the help of Fish and Wildlife Trooper Sergeant Mark Agnew, a pilot and Special Emergency Reaction Team (SERT) sniper. SERT is the trooper equivalent of SWAT. The two would leave predawn, while still dark, on April 30 in a Super Cub from the Wasilla Airport. They planned to survey Buzz's cabin at first light from five-thousand-plus feet in the air to formulate an approach to the cabin. The pair would land on the snow-covered strip behind the lodge. The residents would have a canoe stashed for the two troopers to move across Fish Lakes Creek and they planned to drag it five-hundred-plus yards through the woods to cross the backwater oxbow they used with Helo-1 on the previous day.

Once in place with the terrain surveyed and visual configuration of a landing zone, the two would call on a satellite phone for the SERT team to fly in, remove the two suspects, stabilize the area, and allow the troopers to finish the investigation. With the plan approved, Shanigan and Agnew were fully geared up and took off from the Wasilla airport before 6:00 a.m.

The flight was less than twenty-five minutes northwest to Skwentna. Although spring in Alaska can be sunny and pleasant, this particular morning saw a heavy cloud deck rolling in with temperatures hovering at twenty-eight degrees with forecasted snow. Spring snowstorms in the area are notoriously vicious, leaving Alaskans with a final reminder that winter can happen in all but three months of the year.

After a fast circle around the suspects' cabin, they landed the two-seater Super Cub bush plane on a private gravel landing strip in Skwentna. With the help of a local resident, they waded thigh-deep in rotten snow with plenty of gear as they dragged the canoe through the woods.

After about an hour, they made it to the perimeter of the opening at the cabin. Agnew and Shanigan agreed there weren't many options and approaching from their current position was less than ideal. The plan was to get around to the other side of the cabin where there was a slight elevation with some cover. But, it would take another hour-plus to negotiate the wet ground surrounding much of the log structure because of the flooding conditions worsening daily, as often happens during breakup. There was activity in the cabin. Although the officers could hear music and laughter, it seemed there were only two voices.

After a soaking wet, cold mile and a half approach, the troopers checked in with Command by satellite phone. "We know they're inside, and we're ready to move into position. What do want us to do?" asked Shanigan.

The response was, "Make contact. See if you can get them out. If they don't, we'll cross that bridge as it develops."

Agnew looked at Shanigan and said, "You know they're going to barricade the cabin."

Shanigan replied, "Okay, we have backup ready to go, let's move into position."

Agnew found a meaty cut stump on the small ridge that allowed good visual coverage of the front of the cabin at thirty yards. Shanigan moved down to a lower front corner with just an eight-inch birch tree for cover at an uncomfortable fifteen yards. Agnew said he had Shanigan well covered and the two were ready to reveal their presence.

Shanigan yelled out. "Alaska State Troopers! We need to talk to you!"

The music instantly stopped and silence ensued. Shanigan continued, calmly stating that he needed to speak to the men, and that he was there after speaking to Buzz, their landlord.

Curtains moved and the troopers heard muffled activity coming from inside the cabin. After a couple of minutes of silence, a window opened slowly. Shanigan checked in by radio to make sure Agnew had him covered, and Agnew responded, calm and reassuring—"I got it."

When the window opened, the first response was in a thick New Jersey accent, "Who are you? Fu— you! We're not moving! Hell, we'll burn this place to the ground and shoot you up! You guys have to leave! Go the fu— away!"

Shanigan made it clear they had no plans to leave until they spoke to them, and the banter between the cabin occupants and the troopers continued.

"Okay! You know you're not dealing with Bonnie and Clyde. . . . You're dealing with Clyde and Clyde here! And we have f—ing demands! We want a cell phone and some marijuana!"

Shanigan was feeling highly vulnerable as he assessed he was not in a position for a firefight. The trooper started to signal to Agnew and pretended to be signaling to troopers in other directions so the brothers would believe they were truly surrounded. Although the two troopers didn't know it, the brothers saw a reflection one hundred yards up the hill in the trees. The Jersey Boys thought there was another sniper in the distance. It turned out to be a wind chime on another cabin.

A quick call was placed to the post via the satellite phone to ask for assistance. The two troopers were informed that Helo-1 had been diverted to assist in a rescue for a plane that had crashed during a search and rescue mission that involved life-threatening injuries.

With multiple lives immediately at stake, the two troopers were alone in the Yentna River Valley with backup more than three to four hours away.

Shanigan and Agnew settled in and did their best to help each other keep the conversation going. The Jersey Boys were having more fun, laughing and telling the troopers what they wanted. Shanigan's dialogue was calm, steadfast, and reassuring. Both troopers absolutely knew that they must endure. Their goal was for the two men to come out on their own without discharging a shot. The troopers continued to simulate radio traffic and signals to their ghost SERT team.

Amazingly, in less than an hour, the brothers said they would give up and come out. With Shanigan so close, Agnew assured him over his earpiece that he had these guys covered if anything went wrong.

With clear instructions from Shanigan, the first brother came out the door and slowly walked down the steps with his hands over his head. Assuming a wide stance, he then knelt down in the muck into position to be cuffed with his back and his hands facing the trooper. The second brother was then instructed to come out. Evidently, he was focused on the rifles pointed at him because he walked into the old rail of the porch, broke it, and tumbled off the porch six feet down into the mud. Both brothers found amusement in the fall.

Shanigan lowered his rifle and drew his Glock 40. Both men were on the ground. The brother that plunged off the deck laughed the entire time as he continued to follow the trooper's instruction. With Sergeant Agnew providing cover the entire time, Shanigan holstered his Glock and cuffed both men. Having revealed their presence little more than an hour earlier, the troopers were relieved the two suspects were now in custody.

The two men were moved close to the porch. Although there was no reason to believe anyone else was in the cabin, the troopers wanted to stay out of range of the windows. The troopers could not clear the cabin until they had assistance.

The two brothers were in surprisingly good spirits considering their circumstances. While one trooper was on the phone, the brothers would whisper to the alternate officer and try to convince him to let them go. There were numerous remarks that the two had $700,000 that could be theirs, if the troopers would just leave.

Shanigan and Agnew did their best to keep the prisoners calm and establish a rapport with them for everyone's safety.

Within just a few minutes, the situation became somewhat comfortable and the brothers started to tell stories.

Evidently, the two possessed high criminal self-esteem. "We are the biggest f—ing catch you guys will ever have. We're going to make your careers."

With digital recorders on both officers capturing every word, the brothers went on to tell fragmented details of a crime spree that began in New Jersey. The brothers worked on a construction project together. After one month casing the site, they broke into an office, removed a safe, and hauled it away. When they finally opened it, they found $50,000 in cash and more than $2 million dollars in bonds. This started a crime spree that moved to Florida and then to Puerto Rico. It included kidnapping, home invasions, robbery, drugs, and strippers—lots of strippers. The brothers eventually ended up in Houston, Texas.

Only ten days passed between the first robbery in New Jersey and the crimes they committed in Texas.

With more information and drivers licenses now available, the satellite phone rang with confirmation that these two unfiltered characters were pretty close to the badasses they said they were. There were multiple felony warrants from police departments across New Jersey, Florida, and Puerto Rico.

The brothers believed that Alaska would be the only place in the world where, if they had enough cash, they could hang out, hunt, and fish any time they liked, shoot guns, and live off the grid. No one would ever bother them.

As the stories continued to pile up, one of the brothers complained to the other that he should have never shot up the filter system in the house; the water had become nasty and horrible tasting.

Shanigan knew that if the two brothers were worried about their personal health, they would be far less dangerous to the two troopers that still, as of yet, had no backup, so he gave them a look of horror and asked, "You guys have been drinking untreated water? Do you feel okay? How's your stomach? Do you have a fever?"

It wasn't long before they both subliminally complained of cramps, headaches, and other issues that should stay in the outhouse. Then one brother said in a worried tone, "F——. You mean we have beaver fever! My legs are going numb!"

The troopers just looked at each other, shrugged their shoulders, and stated the obvious: you really don't want to drink the water unless it's filtered.

Then conversations turned to the black-and-white diver (duck) wings tacked up on the porch. Shanigan asked, "Did you guys eat that, too?"

Just then, a magpie (with black-and-white coloring) crossed overhead. Knowing full well that the diver made a less than desirable tasting meal, Shanigan said, "Did it look like that bird that just flew by? Well that's a magpie, man. Did you know those birds consume human feces? If their meat tastes like greasy mud, that can make you real sick, too."

Moans proceeded, followed by more accusatory remarks thrown around about shooting the water system. Why didn't the other brother know enough to not shoot a magpie? God only knows why he was stupid enough to think it was a duck.

Four total hours had passed before they got a call that Helo-1 would soon be en route with a rookie trooper, Hague, taking his first ride on the helicopter to assist.

Just about that time, one of the brothers said he had to pee. Shanigan and Agnew agreed there was no way they were going to unzip the guy and "pull him outside." So, the decision was made to let him piss his pants.

The Jersey fugitive said, "No, no, no! Dude, you've got to help me!"

About that time, Helo-1 showed up with Trooper Hague. The topic of the first discussion was whether to allow the guy to take a leak. No pilot wants anyone to urinate in a three-million-dollar Eurocopter.

With the pilot covering the cuffed, non-peeing brother and Agnew providing outside cover, Hague and Shanigan released the prisoner's arms. The pressure of him kneeling on a stump with three Glock 40s pointed at him at the same time was just too much for the man from New Jersey. As hard as he tried, he could not urinate. He was quickly cuffed again and returned next to his brother.

With backup on the ground, the pilot and Agnew were able to safely cover the two men, allowing Shanigan and Hague to clear the cabin. Inside, the two found a massively disheveled mess with bullet holes everywhere. There were nearly fifty different rifles, shotguns, and handguns. Next to the window, the brothers had stashed hundreds and hundreds of rounds of ammo. A five-gallon bucket alone held an estimated five hundred rounds. There was little question that if the two troopers had not been able to talk the Jersey Boys outside to surrender, Agnew and particularly Shanigan would have truly been in harm's way. The troopers could have never sustained a long firefight with these men.

"It was horribly chilling," Shanigan said.

Since the brothers were claiming that the twenty-two of the guns were, in fact, theirs, the troopers loaded up all the fire-arms in the front seat of the helicopter in two giant black duffle bags. With the brothers sandwiched in the back tightly between Shanigan and Hague, the troopers made sure the two understood the flight rules. Anytime a trooper transports a person on an air-plane, it's made clear that the slightest aggressive behavior will be met with instant deadly force. As Shanigan put it, "We're smart enough to know where we can shoot and not hit the engine. Just sit still and we'll be on the ground in thirty minutes."

Unfortunately, Sergeant Agnew was left to slug his way through the marshy snow muskeg back across the two river crossings to the airstrip and his Super Cub. Shanigan felt bad for the trooper, but the sergeant didn't complain and said, "Don't worry, I love to fly."

While in the air, the two brothers chattered on about dead bodies, killings, kidnappings, and that this arrest was going to make them the most famous criminals of the new millennium.

At the Palmer Airport, a prisoner van took the two into cus-tody and then transported them to the Mat-Su Pre-Trial facility in Palmer. Hague and Shanigan headed back to Talkeetna on the helicopter.

While taking an inventory of all the firearms later that afternoon, the brothers' New Jersey safe heist was confirmed. In addition, Shanigan placed them in Florida from one of the phone numbers they dialed from the cabin.

Within a few hours, cabin owners in the Skwentna area were calling the post, concerned about damage and possibly missing items. Eventually more than one thousand pieces of evidence were logged. Moreover, as suspected, the entire gun cache belonged to the local cabin residents. They had driven snow machines and when the sled either ran out of gas or got stuck, the brothers left them where they died. They then shot them up, but kept the keys with them at the cabin, creating a trophy collection.

The troopers made more than six trips back to Skwentna, amassing hundreds of interviews and phone calls. Massive numbers of digital photos were inventoried. Extensive documentation on the boot prints turned out to be significant in the trial because one pair was unmatched, which made them even easier to identify.

Destruction was everywhere around Buzz's cabin and in many of the others. In some cases, the brothers had sat on the porch of the given structure and shot every small tree they saw until they fell. Many of the yards looked like war zones. Guns were even found in honey buckets buried in human feces.

The swath of destruction was a rough circle with a ten-mile diameter. Within it, as many as twenty-five cabins were ransacked. It is believed that most of the money used in the crime spree was actually from the home invasion and kidnappings in addition to the $50,000 from the initial safe heist in New Jersey. The bonds were cancelled, and therefore, were unable to be cashed.

The two brothers, Jeff Indellicati and Benjamin Cross, were half brothers from the same mother who had been separated in foster care and later adopted by two different families. They reunited as teenagers and told their friends they had plans to burn the world to the ground. The two openly told the troopers they hoped to get fifty years each in prison and were sure they would have a movie deal shortly.

The trial lasted thirty days, with Shanigan testifying for almost five. Massive amounts of evidence were presented and the trial ended with a guilty verdict. The total number of years handed down in the sentence was 180 years for 47 felonies. That translated to 17.5 and 22.5 years.

A few weeks after their arrest, an Alaskan filmmaker interviewed the brothers in jail and they boasted that the two had buried the $700,000 cash from the crime spree on Buzz's property.

In the end, the two brothers' rampage remained isolated because of the lack of cabin dwellers and the break-up weather conditions. When fall transitions to winter, and spring to summer, wilderness residents are forced to stay put for three to four weeks until travel conditions become safe enough to land a plane on the water or use a boat. No one was around to talk about them.

Due to spring breakup, few residents were visiting their cabins, particularly on the weekends. Although the brothers may not have felt their Alaska experience ended well, if they would have run into even a handful of Skwentna locals who understood what was going on, the pair could have easily ended up experiencing Alaskan village justice, which would have equaled the treatment inflicted upon the cabin's water filtration system.

Buzz wrote a letter of apology to every cabin owner with damaged property. To date, the money has never been found.

Barrow Lagoon Rescue

Rescues in Alaska are never typical, especially when they're above the Arctic Circle or at the mouth of the Arctic Ocean.

Point Barrow is the most northern point of America. Yet, it is still 1,100 nautical miles south of the North Pole. Captain Beechey of the British Royal Navy named the village after Admiral Sir John Barrow in 1825.

The village rests with the Chukchi Sea to the west and the Beaufort Sea to the east. Incorporated in 1958, it has 4,429 residents, of which 60 percent are Inupiat Eskimo based on the 2010 Census.

Today, the extreme northern town is a mix of workers that service the North Slope oil fields to the east, plus transportation managers, Eskimo subsistence hunters, fishermen, and numerous traditional Inupiat artisans.

The town made world news during the thirties, when humorist Will Rogers died nearby in a plane crash. And again in the eighties, when the Inupiat Whaling Captains of Barrow— with assistance from Greenpeace, the Alaska National Guard, and the Soviet Navy—helped release a family of gray whales stuck under the ice as depicted in the 2012 movie *Big Miracle*.

It was early winter 1972. On what started out as a typical minus-ten-degree winter afternoon, Trooper Lorry Schuerch was at home and on his lunch break eating chop suey. His radio interrupted the brief respite—someone had driven off the only bridge in town into a lagoon near the medical center. Back in the day, the lagoon was also used as a sewage dump for much of the town. With the EPA not yet established in northern Alaska, many village communities took advantage of ocean bays as sewage storage sites because the extreme, high, thirty-foot tides took the soupy mix out to sea every twelve hours. Today, the town has a modern sewage system.

With a bite of lunch still in his mouth, he ran outside and jumped into his Plymouth Fury cruiser. He arrived at the scene in less than four minutes. As the trooper quickly exited the vehicle, he found the orange painted 2x8 broken rail at the entrance to the small sixty-foot-long bridge. A soaking wet man was sitting with his hands in his face crying. Lying next to him on the ice-covered road was a dead dog. Schuerch could see part of the tailgate of the Chevy pickup poking out of the ice. He asked if there was any one else in the vehicle. The native Eskimo looked up briefly, "Yah! Dougie Edwardson is still inside!" he said, sobbing.

In a moment, the trooper unhooked his gun belt and jumped into the ice-filled water. After recovering from the shock of the low thirties water temperature—it felt like the water was cutting into his skin—he took a deep breath and dove down to the front of the old Chevy. Unable to see, he felt around in the freezing water. Finding the front door open, he put his hand around Dougie's boot and pulled. As hard as the five-foot-six trooper could strain, he could not dislodge the man. He headed back up to the surface for a breath of air.

When he emerged, he saw a large man standing next to the crying passenger and he asked for help. "Get in here! You're tall enough to keep your head above water! I'll put your hand on his boot and then we'll both pull!" yelled the trooper to the six-foot-five man. The man jumped in the malodorous water and shook off the initial cold rush. With another breath, Schuerch reached down, put the boot in the man's hand, and came up for a breath.

Please find our missing child

Amy Patrick 5'3", 105 lbs, blue eyes, 18 years old, born July 20, 1973. She has shoulder length blonde hair.

Last heard from Sunday, September 22nd, approximately 7:00 p.m.

If you have *any* information, please call:
**Alaska State Troopers at
745-2131 or
Crime Stoppers at 745-3333.**

The missing child poster circulated throughout the state of Alaska during the last week of July 1991. Amy was found dead in an Anchorage city landfill on October 26, 1991, near Eagle River, Alaska. *Photographer unknown.*

Trooper Anderson proudly displays his daily headwear cover with his badge. Called "campaign hats" or "lemon squeezers" by the Canadians, the felt circular brim hats have origins that date back before the Civil War. *Photo by the author.*

Trooper Mulvaney leads the Honor Guard during the Fairbanks funeral for slain Troopers Patrick "Scott" Johnson and Gabriel "Gabe" Rich. The two men were killed in the line of duty on May 1, 2014, in Tanana, a village 130 miles north of Fairbanks. *Photo courtesy of the Alaska State Troopers.*

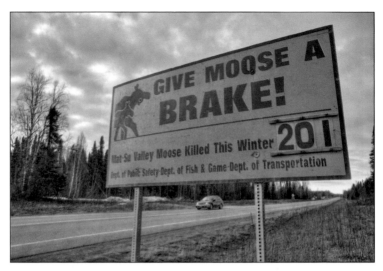

A moose warning sign on the Parks Highway fourteen miles south of Trapper Creek, Alaska. Collisions with moose are one of the most common serious injury accidents on the road network of Alaska. *Photo by the author.*

Trooper Peterson was driving at night on the Seward Highway when a large, dark object fell twenty feet in front of his cruiser: a cow moose believed to have slipped and fallen down the 150-foot roadside cliff. After taking a few photos, the trooper called one of the charities on the Moose List. *Photo courtesy of the Alaska State Troopers.*

Serious vehicle accidents typically come in three circumstances on the two-lane blacktop road system of Alaska; collisions with moose, rollovers, or in this case, a fatal head-on. *Photo courtesy of the Alaska State Troopers.*

Attended by more than fifteen thousand snow machiners and skiers at Summit Lake near Paxton, Alaska, the Arctic Man Ski and Sno-Go Classic sports some of the fastest downhill skiing and snow machining in the world. Troopers Rogers and Simeon take a break on their snow machines. They play a vital role in keeping the event safe and orderly. *Photo courtesy of the Alaska State Troopers.*

Wildlife Trooper Dan Valentine with his patrol truck and ATV. Many troopers are assigned ATVs, snow machines, and boats based on their transportation needs. This photo was taken just days before Trooper Valentine's encounter with more than five hundred pounds of nitroglycerine in Trapper Creek, Alaska. *Photo by the author.*

As part of the Emergency Highway Energy Conservation Act signed into law by President Nixon on January 2, 1974, the state of Alaska received a grant to purchase two *Obey 55* cruisers for traffic control. The vehicles were so unpopular with residents, they were decommissioned and repainted within one year. *Photo courtesy of the Fraternal Order of Alaska State Troopers (FOAST).*

There's a reason Alaskans refer to spring as Break-up. It's a time when river communities are at high risk from dangerous broken ice. Massive ice flows on the Yukon River in 2009 were the size of a home backed into the village of Eagle, destroying everything in its path. *Photo courtesy of the Alaska State Troopers.*

This Cessna 206 floatplane flipped over on the Naknek River outside of King Salmon when it was believed to have struck a fishing boat in 2013. All occupants were safely rescued by nearby fishing vessels. *Photo courtesy of the Alaska State Troopers.*

On December 18, 2007, this Arctic Air Services Cessna 208B turbine departed Bethel Alaska and crashed two miles from the airport. There were two serious injuries; however, all occupants survived. *Photo courtesy of the Alaska State Troopers.*

Taken in the early seventies, this photo shows the bustle of activity when the Alaska Railroad stops in Talkeetna. The small building/loading area is used today for managing heavy freight and repair equipment. A new rail station and ticket office (not shown) were built in the 1990s two hundred yards in the distance. *Photo courtesy of the Talkeetna Historical Society, photographer unknown.*

Sharing office space with a bank and a hardware store across the parking lot, small stations like this one near Talkeetna are common throughout rural Alaska. *Photo by the author.*

During the sixties, not every trooper post had a snow machine or even four-wheel drive pickups. However, the Nome station did. The photo shows Troopers Beauchamp's and Parker's truck and snow-go. The two troopers were the first in the state to have K-9 police dogs. *Photo courtesy of the Fraternal Order of Alaska State Troopers (FOAST), photographer unknown.*

This image shows day hikers on the Ermine Trail to Kesugi Ridge. The Talkeetna Mountain hiking trail can be accessed off the Parks Highway and connects to a network of hundreds of miles of trails in Denali State Park. The area has been the site of numerous rescues, including the Denali State Park bear mauling chronicled in this book. The photo shows a clear day with the Alaska Range and the gray glacial Chulitna River in the background. *Photo courtesy of the Alaska State Troopers.*

The summer of 1981 brought stealthy Detroit iron to chase speeders on the two-lane blacktops of Alaska. Called the Trans Am Enforcement Team, the troopers from right to left include; Darlene Turner, Robert Nesvick, and Oscar Nesvick. *Photo courtesy of the Fraternal Order of Alaska State Troopers (FOAST), photographer unknown.*

Troopers on their way to a community meeting in Kiana. In 1970, the town was the site where three village elders were murdered by a white man during a hunting trip. *Photo courtesy of the Alaska State Troopers.*

For more than fifty years, the Alaska State Troopers and the Royal Canadian Mounted police have held a shooting event to celebrate the camaraderie and cooperation between the two agencies that share more than 1,500 miles of international border. *Photo courtesy of the Alaska State Troopers.*

This government-owned SUV tumbled more than two hundred feet down an embankment on the Taylor Highway near mile 114 into O'Brian Creek during the summer of 2010. The driver, a US Customs Agent, was found one month later at the river's mouth. *Photo courtesy of the Alaska State Troopers.*

Opening day of commercial fishing season brings an impressive array of boats that stay on the ocean for weeks at a time or pursue rogue fisherman at high speeds. Most of this fleet is based on Kodiak Island. In addition to the Super Cub shown, floatplanes are often added to the mix. *Photo courtesy of the Alaska State Troopers.*

Canine Trooper Yukon awaits his turn during a training exercise. Like many police departments, the Alaska State Troopers depend on meticulously trained German Shepherds to seek out suspects in the field. *Photo courtesy of the Alaska State Troopers.*

Schuerch knew he had only been in the water for less than two minutes, but the first clear stages of hypothermia were already visible, including numb hands and shaking. "I tried to pull the second time, but I had no strength left," he recalled.

With the help of the larger man, Dougie Edwardson emerged from the nasty frozen soup of the Point Barrow tidal lagoon. When they pulled Dougie up on to the icy roadbed, he was as blue as a robin's egg.

Dougie was not breathing. In short order, the trooper had his airway cleaned out and was giving him CPR. About thirty seconds later, the small man—who Schuerch had known since high school—puked the rancid water out of his lungs right into the trooper's mouth. With a mouth full of secondary sewage along with the leftover taste of chop suey, Schuerch strained not to lose his own lunch.

Struggling not to regurgitate the composite mix, the trooper gagged, spit, and yelled for water to rinse his mouth out, but there was none. While all this heaving was occurring, a disorientated Dougie sat up and started to yell a litany of curse words at the trooper. A string of sentences bellowed out, including, "He never liked him. How did he get all wet? Why did he smell so nasty?"

They estimated the man was in the sewage lagoon for more than thirteen minutes. And it turned out that Dougie had been highly intoxicated. The combination of the cold water, the lack of struggling, and the aid from Trooper Schuerch and the tall man had saved his life.

About this time, the EMS truck had arrived and they quickly put the ranting, inebriated man on the stretcher amidst his curing and arm waving. The EMS crew slid him into the truck and drove him three hundred yards to the hospital.

Dougie Edwardson made a complete recovery. No charges were ever filed for the man's poor judgment and driving indiscretion.

There had been little thanks to the trooper for his efforts in the cold, sewage bath that day. However, at a dinner years later,

Dougie Edwardson told Schuerch's son Tony: "Please thank your dad. I would have never lived another minute without his help."

Schuerch said that was good enough for him. But he admitted that he was never able to eat chop suey again.

Rubber Gloves, a VW Bus, and a House Coat

No matter the community, the mundane tasks associated with police work can try the patience of any officer. This can be especially true during the high school graduation season in a small town.

Trooper Dallas Massie was working patrol during a hiatus from ongoing investigations. It was a Friday night in 1996 when the Wasilla, Palmer, and Big Lake high school graduations converged. There were high expectations for raucous teenage behavior, as the rights of passage for a few thousand seniors besieged the small towns in an area that's often called The Valley.

The Mat-Su Valley communities sit north of Anchorage across the Knick Arm Bridge that splits two highways, the Glenn to the east and the Parks to the west, and then heads to the north toward Fairbanks. The towns are at the base of two mountain ranges, the Chugach, along the Glenn Highway to the east, and the Talkeetna Mountains to the north.

Part of the Mat-Su Borough, the area has close to eighty-nine thousand residents, based on information from the 2010 Census. During the nineties, this number most likely hovered around fifty thousand. Although it's similar to any-town America, true wilderness lies just outside the city limits and may include grizzly bears, moose, and salmon gathering in almost every stream during the summer.

Trooper Massie had the temperament to deal with over-zealous teenagers. He was known for his calm demeanor when Alaskans were straddling the lines or hovering a bit over the edge. He liked to frequent large party areas. Once there, he politely made his presence known. He made it clear that anyone who left any party drunk and then tried to drive would be taking a ride in the back of his Dodge cruiser and charged with DWI.

Although the trooper was always friendly, all the teens knew they would indeed make a trip to the jail in Palmer if they challenged the officer's authority behind the wheel.

The trooper was deliberately heading to one of the largest party zones in a gravel pit. His overt goal was to be observed by the graduating high schoolers. This particular part of Palmer rests at the base of Hatcher's Pass. The majestic pass is known for its massive twenty-plus-foot snow falls on its steep terrain. It has an abandoned gold mine, an old lodge from the twenties, and sweeping views that attract tourists in the summer. The sheer rock face goes straight down the mountain to the hay-farming valley below. The views are nothing short of spectacular, and everyone in town knows that the pass is only open from the first of July to the first of October.

During the last week of May, most Alaskans are ready to cut loose. Daylight now stretches for nearly twenty hours each day and twilight doesn't truly lead to darkness. As Massie pulled into party central at the base of the Talkeetna Mountains, he witnessed at least two hundred kids quickly trying to hide the beer in their hands. The bonfire roared and the music blared around them.

Although the area didn't go silent when the trooper arrived, half the kids did make an effort to look bored as they tried to act as though there was nothing to celebrate. Despite the bonfire that raged twenty feet in the air, the gathering in the gravel pit seemed reasonably calm.

While the trooper was talking to one group and reminding them not to head out on the highway if they have had anything drink, a dispatch came over the radio. The call entailed an elderly woman driving erratically in a Volkswagen Vanagon camper bus wearing just rubber gloves and bathrobe.

The call also stated that she was behaving erratically, going as far as knocking on residents' doors and trying to run drivers off the road.

The trooper was admittedly confused at the report. When one of the teens said, "Hey, what's that?" Massey abruptly turned around to see a VW Vanagon bus heading straight toward his cruiser. Around him, teens cheered.

The elderly, rubber-glove-and-bathrobe-clad lady passed the cruiser at forty miles hour, throwing gravel on the state trooper's hood and against his windshield.

"The kids went insane," said Massey.

Amid cheering from the two hundred teenagers, the VW Bus made a sharp turn and headed back out the gravel pit to Palmer Fishhook Road. With lights and siren on, the trooper chased the seventy-year-old-plus senior citizen at relatively high speed toward the mountain range. He easily caught up to her.

"After all, it was a VW bus," said Massey.

At first the trooper thought if he moved up on the driver's side, he could get her to pull over. The trooper's Dodge cruiser moved to the side, signaling the woman to move over. Then the lady swerved into the trooper's lane and forced the car back behind her bus.

"There was no way I was going to let this old lady put a dent in my cruiser. I would never hear the end of it at the office. And the paperwork that would follow would make it less than ideal," said Massey.

It seemed apparent the only way to deal with the rubber-fisted VW driver was to back off and to keep the lights and siren on. His strategy was to wait her out and keep the elderly lady and himself out of harm's way.

Massey kept dispatch informed of their location as the woman passed the last turn off heading up the mountain to Hatcher's Pass. "What is she thinking? Everyone knows the pass is closed by a wall of snow just past the mine," the trooper thought. Massey gave the woman even more room, yet kept her in sight. She had boxed herself in. There was no place to go, and there were no turn-offs except for a few parking lots.

"I didn't want to be the reason that the VW went tumbling down one of the many parts of the road that had no guardrails and steep dropoffs," said the trooper.

When the VW got to the historic mine site, Massey hoped she would pull into the parking lot where he could block off the entrance and wait her out. As it turned out, all the entrances were already blocked. Surrounded by deep snow on the sides of the road, the woman simply slowed to a stop at the gate.

Massey had no plans to wrestle a lady in a bathrobe out of her van. He blocked the van in tightly, and with no place to go, the woman shut the engine off upon the trooper's request.

Massey could see the woman's lips moving rapidly. She was speaking aimlessly and not making sense. Though she was not able to address the trooper directly, she did get out of the van, as instructed. However, she also expressed, in no uncertain terms, that she wasn't leaving her van or going with the trooper.

In an act of defiance, she then sat down in a pothole filled with ice-crusted water. She said that she would sit there all night until the trooper went away.

The woman was clearly in a state of confusion and the veteran trooper did not want to upset her further. So he calmly said, "Tell you what. Let's just stay here until you're ready to get into my nice, warm cruiser. It's really warm in there."

At this juncture, the trooper thought she may have told him to kiss her ass, but he wasn't absolutely certain. The trooper had already called for a wrecker to impound the van. He waited patiently and the woman insisted she could stay as long as she had to.

"I was just not going to physically engage the lady unless she gave me no choice. However, I was amazed she was willing to sit in a cold, icy puddle for more than fifteen minutes," said Massey.

With the clock ticking into what the officer felt was getting to be a somewhat dangerous period of time, the woman suddenly changed her tone. Massey could see the lights of the wrecker two thousand vertical feet down along the pass road. Tersely, she acknowledged she was starting to feel like maybe she could sit in the car and warm up—with one caveat. She requested the trooper let her go back to sit in the icy puddle once she was warm.

Massey said, "Sure. Let's get you warmed up and we'll talk about it."

The woman continued to mumble quietly to herself as Massey sat her in the front seat of the car. He quietly and casually mentioned that she was under arrest for reckless driving and that she may be more comfortable with a set of handcuffs on. The lady said okay, and Massey gently put a set of cuffs around her wrists and in front of her body while she sat in the front seat.

The woman was subdued in the car, probably because she was feeling better with the heat blasting at her. Little was said when the wrecker arrived to impound the VW, and Massey turned the car around. He quietly headed back to Palmer to the jail that, at that time, was in the basement of the Palmer City Hall.

The trooper gave her his coat for the ride down the mountain. Twenty minutes later, he was helping the lady down the police office steps.

As Massey took the lady into the waiting room, the woman saw the dispatcher and yelled, "He raped me!"

The dispatcher gave Massey a confused look and vehemently shook his head no.

Massey told the woman, "Well, let's just find a nice spot here and make you comfortable."

The woman would be arraigned first thing in the morning.

As she calmed down, the woman decided the dispatcher had not raped her. Massey then asked, "How did you know I wasn't going to run you off the road?"

In a moment of absolute clarity, the woman piped up and said, "Please. I know you guys. You hate to ding those police cars and fill out all that paperwork."

With the elderly woman settled in, Massey finished his shift by returning to the city hall for the woman's morning arraignment. He learned this was not her first reckless driving charge. A week earlier, she led the Anchorage PD on a chase down the Seward Highway all the way to Girdwood, fifteen miles south out of town. During the previous chase, she had driven the vehicle off the road into a patch of devil's club, Alaska's notorious thorny plant. That was why she was wearing rubber gloves—medicated salve now covered her hands.

Everyone in the courtroom was relieved when her husband arrived. The man was dressed as if he were attending an English country event, in a tweed jacket and a Burberry bow tie. A slight man, no more than five feet in stature, he calmly assured the judge that his wife would get a psychiatrist's help immediately. He promised he would take time off from his job as a driving instructor to make sure she had the help she needed.

Massey and the district attorney agreed that the charges should be dropped, and the woman was released into the custody of her husband, the driving instructor.

The Cessna Tow

If you operate a boat in a river or in the heavy tidal seas of Alaska, experiencing a complete loss of power is one of the worst and most dangerous events that could occur.

Trooper Jeff Babcock was working his normal license check of fishermen between Cordova and Valdez. Like all Alaska Wildlife Troopers, the sergeant stops hunters, anglers, and commercial fishermen to check their game and licenses and perform an inspection of their vessels. What was different about Babcock's mode of transportation, though, was that he traveled almost exclusively by air, weather permitting.

In the summer of 1988, Babcock was flying a blue and white Cessna 182 on floats marked with trooper insignias.

"People are really shocked when they are running a boat in Prince William Sound, haven't seen another vessel of any kind, and then, all of a sudden, a float plane shows up, circles, lands, and docks against the boat with a request to come aboard," said Babcock, smiling.

On this particular day on the coast of Prince William Sound, Babcock was in the air, the weather was clear, the sea was calm, and the temperature was warm.

As the trooper banked the Cessna toward the entrance to Valdez, he flew between Bligh Island and Glacier Island. Looking down, he could see a semi-rigid inflatable without an outboard motor cover. Upon closer inspection, the only person in the boat was hopelessly paddling on the bow.

The trooper lowered the float plane's altitude to five hundred feet and covered a large circle around the boat. In response, the passenger gave the international boating distress signal; he outstretched his arms to each side and slowly raised and lowered them repeatedly.

Babcock quickly checked for wind and was able to set the float plane smoothly on the water. He idled the plane toward the boat to prevent any wake.

Once the trooper was sure the drift would intercept the boat, he killed the engine to stop the propeller. Then he opened the door and got out on the float. The location was less than one mile from the same reef that damaged the Exxon Valdez on March 24, 1989.

The man in the Zodiac was covered in sweat and his clothes were soaked. "Hey, thanks for stopping," he said. Babcock asked what the problem was, and the man said, "I have no idea, the engine just stopped and she won't start back up. I know I have gas."

The man said that the boat belonged to Stan Stephens of Stan Stephens Glacier & Wildlife Cruises, an ocean tour operator who owned a lodge on the other side of Glacier Island, fifteen miles to the northwest.

As the plane drifted to the Zodiac, the man threw the trooper a line. As the two men talked, a distressing thought crossed Babcock's mind. He knew the Coast Guard was on a call almost eighty miles away. The first check on the radio found not one fishing boat particularly close to the man in the raft.

"I can't leave you out here drifting," said the trooper. Babcock knew that a violent, outgoing tide would have the man and his inflatable zipping through the Hinchinbrook Strait into the Gulf of Alaska in less two hours. Once in the open gulf, the boat and driver would be in true peril and would then need a Coast Guard rescue.

From a resource and safety standpoint, the trooper could not leave the driver of the boat. Because he borrowed the boat from Stephens, the man was not willing to get into the plane with Babcock and leave it.

"Stan would kill me if I abandoned his boat! I'll take my chances in the Straits and into the Gulf and see if anyone can tow me in."With the tide ripping out at a constant speed of ten knots, even if Stan could be reached by radio, it was unlikely a boat would catch the Zodiac before it was adrift in the Gulf.

Babcock ran several rescue scenarios in his head before a viable option surfaced. "I'll tell you what. How about letting me tow you and the boat to Glacier Island?" he asked.

Confused, the man looked at the trooper, squinted his eyes a few times, cocked his head to one side, and said, "How are you going to do that that?"

Scratching his head, Babcock said, "I have a long grab rope on the tail to catch the plane when I dock. Let's hook it up to the Zodiac, and I'll tow you to Glacier Island. Once I get back up in the air, I'll radio Stan and let him know he'll need to come and get you. At any rate, this boat's floating out to sea. Once we get you to the island, you'll only be thirty to forty minutes from the lodge," said the trooper.

"Is this even legal? Will the FAA allow you to do this?" the man said skeptically.

"Hmmmm . . . probably not, but do you want to keep floating out to sea or do you want to get home tonight?" asked Babcock.

Although troopers try to abide by FAA articles that encompass many of the rules that would likely find this kind of rescue questionable, like the military, the troopers are listed as "Public Use." This designation allows them a wider berth with more latitude and freedom when executing rescue operations.

The trooper climbed up into the Cessna and fired up the engine. Babcock was fully aware he wouldn't be able go much faster than idle. However, he was a little surprised by just how bad the prop-wash was. Quickly throttling down, the Cessna was on its way across the bay in the outgoing tide. It took the trooper more than two hours of dodging calved ice from the Columbia Glacier to cross the opening to the outer east side of Glacier Island.

Babcock checked with the man, who had now disconnected the boat from the plane and was comfortably anchored to the rocky beach. Babcock yelled at the man, "I'll call Stan on the radio and tell him where you are. You'll be out of here in two or three hours."

With a wave and a slam from the Cessna door, the 182 throttled up and in short order was back in the air heading back to Cordova.

With more than five different kinds of radios on the plane, Babcock said his wing looked like a pincushion. Because he had so many different kinds of antennas, he was able to reach Stan at the lodge.

"Hi Stan, this is Trooper Babcock. I just rescued one of your Zodiacs and it's sitting on the east side of Glacier Island with its driver,"

"Wow! That's great! Is everything okay?" Stephens asked.

Babcock replied, "The driver is fine. You'll just need to go out and tow him back. It was no problem."

Stephens pushed the button on the marine radio mic and asked, "I don't want to sound ungrateful, but I'm absolutely swamped up here at the lodge. It will be about four or five hours before we can get out there. Could you at least tow him to the mouth of Growler Bay? That way it will only be a twenty-five-minute pick up. It's on your way back to Cordova . . . Over."

Babcock realized then that Stephens had no idea that he was in a plane. He responded, "Negative. I'm already in the air."

"Yeah, but you said you towed him, right?" said Stephens incredulously.

"That's right, I did," responded Babcock.

Stephens had evidently pushed the button of the mic, held it down, and forgotten to release it. In the background, Babcock could hear ongoing conversations as Stephen talked back and forth with a bevy of people. They were saying things like, "That's impossible!" "How the . . . did he do that?" "What did he say he did?" "Where is he?"

Undeterred, Babcock repeated, "That's right, I'm in a Cessna 182." Babcock could still hear in the conversations in the background and then he heard the sound of roaring laughter.

Stephens came back on the mic and said, "Wow, Trooper, you've certainly had enough fun for one day. We copy. We'll go get the Zodiac immediately. Now I think I've heard it all. Safe travels, Trooper. Over and out."

Babcock was feeling pretty resourceful. He was only slightly worried about what his commander would say when he read the day's activity report. But the trooper knew that even a reprimand wouldn't have stopped him from rescuing and preventing a man in a motorless craft from drifting alone into the Gulf of Alaska.

The next day, after his commander read the day's report, Babcock was called into the office. "Did you really tow a boat fifteen miles across Prince William Sound with the Cessna? That can't be legal with the FAA!" barked the post commander.

Babcock's response was, "Sir, yes I did."

The commander just smiled, shook his head, and said, "Good job, Trooper. Now, get out my office."

The Kobuk River Caribou Killings

Cultural disparities are unfortunate parts of coexistence when native and white communities merge. In Alaska, rural subsistence living is constantly at odds with state and federal agencies and visiting whites.

Even basic communication can result in conflict; white guests are often confused and offended by the lack of conversation common in many Eskimo exchanges and Eskimos often feel that whites display entitlement or attitudes with boasting loud conversation.

On the afternoon of January 25, 1970, FAA employee Harold Lie was flying a local physician on a wolf-hunting trip over the Kobuk River. Lowering the ski-equipped Cessna to just two hundred feet off the snow, the two men spotted a man holding his hands over his head as though he were surrendering. When the Cessna flew directly over him, the desperate-looking man collapsed into the snow.

The pilot quickly turned the Cessna and was able to land the plane on the river just few yards from where the man was standing. The exhausted young man got up and struggled to walk toward the idling plane. With the side door open and the plane idling, the physician helped the young white man into the back of the plane. The man breathed heavily and looked cold and disheveled.

He said he was traveling in a hunting party of four men and was the lone survivor of the group. The bodies were miles away back at their camp, up the Kobuk River. The young man, who they could now see looked like a teenager, said he had walked all night in the minus-forty-degree temperatures, trying to make it back to Kiana. After telling them this story, he passed out.

With the unconscious man clearly in the moderate stages of hypothermia and possibly frostbitten, Lie immediately headed back to the village landing in Kiana where the man was taken to the local native clinic and left in the care of a nurse.

Lie sent word via radio to State Trooper Bob Boatright in nearby Kotzebue that he had found a white man alone on the river. He told Boatright there had been a murder up the river. With the young man being treated and just a few hours of daylight left, the pilot flew back up the Kobuk River with a sense of urgency. With the sun low in the horizon, Lie saw a camp in the distance and lowered the plane altitude to see if there were indeed no survivors. As the pilot circled the disheveled camp in the snow, he identified only one body lying in front of the tent. No one emerged from the tent despite Lie's several minutes in the area. Although he couldn't be sure, there appeared to be no signs of life. With the sun down below the horizon, the pilot had to get back before the twilight ended. He turned the Cessna back to Kiana.

Kiana is located on the banks of the Kobuk River at the confluence of the Squirrel River. In 1928, the average yearly population was 98 and, as of 2010, the number of recorded inhabitants was 361. Its residents are mostly Kowagmiut Inupiat Eskimos who have used the area for thousands of years. The village's first contact with whites was as recent as 1898, and more settlers arrived by boat in the summer of 1901. During Alaska's territorial period, a post office was established in the village by 1915. Mail was delivered once a month in the summer and would arrive by dogsled from Fairbanks with slightly greater frequency during the winter months. In 1964, the village became part of the Northwest Arctic Borough. The town is about forty miles upriver from the mouth of the Hotham Inlet, a large bay that passes by the larger town of Kotzebue, another fourteen miles away by boat.

Today, the mostly native population continues to strive for a subsistence lifestyle in which they live on moose, caribou, waterfowl, berries, sheefish, and chum salmon. Red Dog Mine, one of the largest open pit mines in the world, employs many villages and, like many villages in northern Alaska, is located on the North Slope in the oil fields to the east.

Within an hour, Trooper Boatright and Chief of Police Stevens of Kotzebue had arrived in the darkness, unable to check the camp up the Kobuk River. So the first stop was the clinic to see the survivor, who was now conscious and in improving condition. The two officers sat down to interview the Caucasian nineteen-year-old man, who had by now identified himself as Norman Leroy Johnson.

Johnson's father was a foreman for the Alaskan Housing Authority responsible for building new housing in local bush communities. The young man's father had arranged with several locals for his son Leroy to accompany a group of men for a caribou hunt. During the interview, the officers learned that the deceased men's names in the camp were Freddy Jackson, Oscar Henry, and Clarence Arnold—all Eskimos from Kiana. The young man told them an Eskimo wearing a hat that said BUTCH massacred the men in the camp. Johnson agreed to stay in the clinic and wait for his father to arrive from Kotzebue the following morning.

The Camp

The next morning, the two officers arranged for a Cessna 206 to fly up from Kotzebue to Kiana and wait on standby to transport the bodies. The two officers left Kiana in twilight to investigate the scene with their bush pilot. Stahlei, their pilot, set the plane down two miles away so Boatright and Stevens were able to enter the camp on foot and make sure no other threats existed.

The two officers covered the terrain quickly and approached the camp from raised snow burms on the river. As they glassed the camp from behind, they knew no one was alive and they could see one body lying in front of the tent. Boatright radioed the plane and they entered the disheveled camp careful not to disturb any of the existing foot or snow machine tracks that could later be used as evidence.

The camp consisted of a single eight-by-ten-foot canvas tent set up fifty yards from the river's north side.

A well-worn snow machine trail stretched from the river to the camp and off into the interior up along river. An additional circling track left the main trail and made a loop around the camp. Two snow machines—an Arctic Cat and a Johnson Challenger—with the gear sleds connected were still in the camp. The Arctic Cat was half full of fuel and the start switch was in the off position.

Other gear on the sleds included .243-caliber Winchester, camping gear, and rope. The firearm was secured to the machine and wrapped in burlap with a rope. A vintage, well-used .30-06 Springfield rifle was leaning on a set of fuel cans with two rifle casings, one a .30-06 and the other a .30-30. Multiple, gutted caribou were strung close by and a cased Model 94 lever action Winchester that had blood spattering on the outside of the case and a box of .30-30 ammunition were also in range.

The man lying on his stomach in front of the tent was Frederick Jackson. He had suffered multiple gunshot wounds, but in the minus-forty-below temperatures, the frozen blood all over his jacket made it difficult to determine just how many times and where he had been shot. Bloodstains leading into the tent indicated that the man was shot inside the tent and had stumbled out.

Inside the tent lying face-down on the floor next to a dislodged camp stove was the body of Clarence Arnold. Like Jackson, it was difficult to tell how many times the man had been shot because the pooling blood had frozen. Arnold appeared to be frozen to the ground. At the rear of tent lay Oscar Henry, still holding on to his pants as if he were pulling them up when he was shot. He had also sustained several blows to the head from a heavy object.

Multiple bullet holes pierced through the tent and even the teapot had rounds through it. The tent as much of the outside was disheveled and in a state of chaos.

Because of the changing trajectory of the bullets entering the tent at four feet and exiting at one, Boatwright was sure the bullets were shot outside the tent from a standing position. Numerous boot tracks surrounded the outside of the tent and there were shell casings both inside and outside the tent that included .270 rounds. A matching rifle was not found at the scene.

The snow machine tracks indicated that a different sled—an Evenrude—had been at the scene. The sled had made a circle around the camp and then departed on the main trail in the direction of Ambler, a village up the Kobuk River toward the interior.

In The Village

After four hours, the sun set and the two officers completed the preliminary investigation and loaded the bodies on the transport sleds. They would tow the bodies by snow machine to an area ten miles away where the 206 Cessna could land to recover them. The bodies were flown back to Kiana for the inquest and would later be flown to Anchorage for examination by the Coroners. The two officers went back to Kiana to organize a search party and request further assistance from the Fairbanks Post.

It was not surprising to find tensions high in the village, as literally everyone had now heard different stories about the killings. Small, rural Alaskan villages are tightly knit, with many or most of the Inupiat residences related to one another. People were clearly upset, to say the least, that three well-respected men from the village had been murdered.

Both the locals and the troopers believed no one of Eskimo blood would or could ever commit such a violent crime. The groups were suspicious of the white man, Johnson, the only survivor. Boatwright and Stevens were cautious of the boy's story.

With Boatright's initial investigation of the site complete, a group of residents would search the trail and go over the camp the next morning. When they reached the camp, one of the ten men on the team, a Kiana resident named Sam Reed, noticed footprints leading away from the main trail and along the river to a small snow bank. They brushed the snow away to find a Winchester .243 bolt-action rifle with the bolt missing and the stock buttplate with the lower end of the wood covered in frozen blood.

The group was convinced the pattern of footsteps meant the tracks were made by someone who had been walking a while and not someone who had climbed off a snow machine to stash the rifle.

Send Help

As rumor and animosity flowed freely through Kiana, Boatright called the Fairbanks Post and requested the help of Trooper Lorry Schuerch—the first Inupiat Eskimo to attend the Trooper Academy in Sitka in 1968. Not only was Trooper Schuerch an Eskimo, but he was also raised in Kiana and would be indispensable in the investigation and communicating with the residents.

When the request came into the Fairbanks Post, Trooper Schuerch was on patrol and had been called back to the station to meet with his supervisor, Sergeant Al Hume. The supervisor knew chances were high that at least one of the murder victims would likely be a direct or distant relative of the trooper.

"Lorry, we have some bad news for you," Hume said. "There's been a triple homicide in your village and things are getting bad. There's talk of an insurrection and suspicions are high that a white kid may have killed the three men. I really need someone who understands the community and can keep this from getting out of hand. I would hate to see some of these people take the law into their own hands and then have to pay a horrible price. I want to send you to Kiana to help Trooper Boatright."

Schuerch immediately replied, "Yes, I'll be ready as soon as I can."

In just a few hours, Schuerch was on his way by air to Kotzebue and then to Kiana. By this time, the bodies were en route with Trooper Boatright. Leroy Johnson and his father were on their way to Anchorage where investigative troopers would interview the boy again as soon as they arrived.

The Second interview

With the boy's father now present, Boatright and Stevens interviewed Leroy Johnson again.

Evidently, the boy's father had set up the hunt for his son and over the Christmas holidays, Mr. Johnson had given Leroy a brand new Winchester .30-30 lever action rifle for the occasion. The young Leroy Johnson arrived in Kiana on January 21. Residents were happy to set up the hunt for Mr. Johnson's son; his job made him an important man in the village, a man responsible for many discussions about new homes for the community. Mr. Johnson's lead carpenter, Freddy Jackson, would join Leroy on the hunt. On the morning of January 23, the two men set out on a single snow machine toward Ambler. The temperature was cold, nearing fifty below.

According to younger Johnson, they arrived at a single tent camp and Clarence Arnold and Oscar Henry were already there. They would spend the night and hunt as a group the following day. Later in the afternoon, another Eskimo from Ambler named Clarence Wood stopped at the camp and had dinner with the group.

According to Boatright, during the interview the boy said there were no arguments or disagreements in the camp. Leroy did mention that the Eskimos spoke in Yupik and he didn't understand the conversation nor was he included in the dialogue.

After dinner, Wood left on his snow machine and headed toward Ambler. The men got ready to go to bed. Johnson recalled they were getting into their sleeping bags when he heard a snow machine approach and then stop outside the tent.

The young man stated the other Eskimos went outside to meet the man in the deep cold. Johnson provided a detailed description of the visiting Eskimo's clothing and size, stating, "I would definitely recognize him again."

With Johnson in his sleeping bag and the men outside, the boy was sure an argument started. "I could tell when they started arguing because they raised their voices and got real loud. Then the guy started up his machine and it sounded like he was driving away . . . then I heard the engine stop."

Boatright asked, "So then what happened?"

"Well," said Johnson, "two of the men, Henry and Arnold, came in to the tent and climbed into their sleeping bags. Then there were several shots! I remember hearing 'No! No!' That's all I heard. Clarence Jackson was evidently hit first and fell in the back of the tent where I was in my sleeping bag."

Johnson said that he was able to crawl out of his bag, slip under the tent, and run to a bush and hide. "From there, I could see this guy firing two large and small caliber weapons. Then he stopped. I saw him go into the tent and come out again in a couple of minutes. The shooter then walked around the tent and got on his snow machine and headed toward Kiana. I waited until the machine sound disappears and then I went back to the tent to grab my gear. Everyone was dead. I looked for a weapon but the rifles I found were all empty. And the guns that were on the sleds outside were gone. I kept looking and finally found my Winchester, but it was empty."

Johnson went on to say that he tried to start one of the snow machines only to find it wouldn't run. "I was afraid the man would come back. I wanted to get out of there, so I left without even my Winchester because I had no bullets for it."

Leroy Johnson then headed into the Arctic night at minus forty and trekked more than thirty-eight miles until, exhausted and cold, the Cessna found him with his hands in the air and picked him up.

Johnson added, "I didn't shoot those men! And I can identify the man who did!"

Boatright absolutely considered the young man a suspect; he was uncomfortable with the boy's account and saw numerous holes in his story. He also sincerely believed that an Eskimo just didn't have the predisposition to sensibly kill another. The only possible way the story may have been true would have been if the mystery killer man was intoxicated. But Johnson hadn't given him a reason to think this angry gun-wielding murderer, who acted with such aggressive cold-blooded control, could have been drinking.

With tensions so high in the community, Boatright told the father and son to leave immediately and instructed them to meet with investigative troopers.

With Johnson's departure, Boatright's investigation went into high gear expecting the arrival of Trooper Lorry Schuerch. The trooper contacted the village council members, post masters, schoolteachers, and VPOs of Kiana—Noorvik, Ambler, and Selawik—to identify any hunters who were out during the time in question. Boatright found that only thirteen men were out hunting and their stories checked out: they all were hunting in groups of three to four men.

Boatright left for Kotzebue and then Kiana, where he would meet Schuerch and have have better communications with the Anchorage investigators. Schuerch's presence would surely aid in calming the village residents.

A Calming Influence

Schuerch could feel the tension in the air when he arrived in Kiana. His first stop after the VPOs office was to see his father at the trading post. His father always seemed to have the pulse of what was going on in the village. "My father told me one of the sons of the slain men said, in the presence of others, that he was going kill every white man in the village," recalled Schuerch.

The threatening man was Schuerch's cousin, Paul. In just ten minutes after hearing this news from his father, the trooper was standing on his cousin's porch and knocking on the door. The man answered the door and let in the trooper.

Paul and the young trooper sat in silence in the living room for a while. Paul drank whiskey. Schuerch finally said, "Paul, you're going about this the wrong way. I don't want to see anything bad happen to you. Let me just take your guns and put them away in storage and you just take it easy and don't hurt anyone."

Little else was said, so when Paul nodded his head, the trooper picked up all of his rifles and took them to his cousin's mother's house. The firearms were wrapped in cloth and locked in an outdoor fish cache that the family used for their salmon. Schuerch never heard of any problems concerning Paul and there was never an assault on any of the white residents of Kiana.

Schuerch went on to visit other village elders and family members of the slain victims to help settle the communities and assure them that the troopers would find the killer and bring him to justice.

Tensions were so extreme that the principal of the school wanted to evacuate the teachers and students because he feared for his and their lives. Schuerch's presence was a calming force in the village and the troopers gave him credit for keeping the village from an all-out insurrection.

Boatright asked Schuerch to organize another group of villagers to follow the trail away from Kiana the next morning to check the now dismantled camp and interview possible witnesses to activities before and after the crime. Boatright also asked that Schuerch interview Clarence Wood—the only possible witness or suspect based on Johnson's statement.

The group of six men left for Ambler on three snow machines. They spent the night at a white family's home in a spruce sod-covered twelve- by sixteen-foot cabin similar to traditional buildings of several hundred years ago. With the near-sixty-below temperatures chilling the night air, the six men were relieved to spend the night inside next to the wood stove and on the spruce and willow branch floor. Trooper Schuerch brought a care package prepared by his mother in Kiana for the occasion. It contained Oreo cookies for the cabin owners and their children.

One of the reasons the group stopped at the home was because the cabin was on the main trail for the Kobuk River and anyone coming back from the camp where the incident occurred would have surely been heard by the residents.

The next morning, Schuerch found Clarence Wood. Wood was anxious to talk to the trooper and, although he didn't know any of the details about the killings, he was able to fill in some of what had happened at the camp. The interview with the trooper was conducted using the Yupik language.

As Johnson stated, Clarence Wood said he had stopped at the camp. The thirty-two-year-old Eskimo said he left Kiana the morning of the murders planning on going hunting with Jackie Johnson. On the way to Ambler, Jackie had a faster machine and Wood never caught up to him and instead stopped when he came to the Kiana hunters' tent.

"When I arrived around 7:00 p.m., Henry and Arnold were doing camp work, chopping wood and carrying ice for water. Oscar invited me into the tent and led the way, moving slow because he has terrible arthritis. I saw the white sitting on a grub box inside near the wood stove. Being that the kid was in the way, Oscar asked him to move and he went over to his sleeping bag and crawled into it. We had coffee, and they asked me to stay for supper."

The men welcomed the resident and shared the stew made from tongue, heart, and liver, the best traditional parts of the caribou. During the interview with Schuerch, Wood said that Leroy Johnson barely said a word and was "real mopey." Speaking in Yupik, the Kiana hunters told Wood that the boy had fallen off the sled, walked ten miles to the site of the hunt, and had not been able to take part.

After dinner, Wood was due back in Ambler twenty-five miles away and needed to leave. He left on his snow machine and drove off into the night, using the main trail up the Kobuk River.

Wood arrived in Ambler that night and left the following morning, heading to his camp at Selawik, to the southeast, where he heard there was better hunting. In Selawik, twenty-four hours after he had dinner in the tent camp, Wood heard over the radio about the killings. He thought, "I was just there, how could that be?"

Wood immediately left the camp in the morning and went back to Ambler and then on to Kotibue to find out the details of what had happened to his friends.

The Interrogation

On January 26 at 11:30 p.m., the Johnsons arrived in Anchorage. Trooper Corporal Ule "Dean" Bivins met the two at the airport, where he took the initial statement. The pair was instructed to be at the trooper's office in the morning. Bivins recalled that after the interview at the airport, he thought the boy was honest and he didn't suspect the young man. The story seemed consistent with the report he had received; however, when Bivins called Tom Anderson, sergeant of the Anchorage investigative unit, to set up the interview, Anderson relayed to Bivins that he had just spoken to Boatright and the trooper told the commander that evidence continued to mount against Johnson. It looked as though the boy had committed the murders and Clarence Wood was innocent. Boatright said, "There was no Eskimo killer. It was Johnson."

Sergeant Anderson, Corporal Bivins, and Sergeant Bill Nix met the Johnsons the next morning at the trooper station in Anchorage. The interview took place in a room with two-way glass and was the very first video-taped interrogation the Alaska State troopers had ever performed.

Nix had served at the Kotzebue Post and was familiar with Eskimo culture and traditions. The three agreed it was time to pressure Johnson and challenge his story for the first time.

"Johnson didn't seem comfortable or sure of himself. We knew that if he was guilty, the truth would come pretty fast," said Anderson.

Bivins and Nix sat across from the suspect. Nix never dropped eye contact when he said, in an aggressive tone, "You're a liar! No

Eskimo did that shooting! The evidence doesn't fit and there are holes all over your story! These people could never commit such a vicious crime! Tell me the truth!"

Fewer than two minutes from the start of Trooper Nix's interrogation, Leroy Johnson solemnly looked down at the table and said, "I'm the one who shot Freddy, Clarence, and Oscar. I got up to take a leak and just picked up a rifle and fired it seven times into the tent. Then I picked up Freddy's gun and fired it until it was empty as well. Somebody came out of the tent and I shot him once and he fell in front of the entrance. After I stopped firing, I went inside to get my clothes . . . the bedrolls and everything was all spread over and it was full of smoke. One of them was lying on his back and the other was just inside the entrance. The third man was outside. I tried to start one of the snow machines, but couldn't, so I grabbed a rifle and started walking. It was Freddy gun and along the trail I buried it in the snow. I don't know what my intentions were when I started shooting into the tent . . . I just started firing."

Johnson went on to say that he didn't see the men in the tent when he shot them. He only saw Freddy Jackson, who stumbled outside the tent. He didn't have any animosity toward the Eskimos he murdered.

In an interview twenty years later, Bivins said, "I think Johnson felt completely alone and helpless out there and he simply went berserk. He didn't have any business being in there in the first place and with everyone speaking Eskimo, it heightened his fears of being defenseless and alone."

The Mind of the Killer

Interviews and court statements revealed a clearer picture of Johnson's anger and sense of isolation the night of the murders.

On the hunt day, the group moved ahead on the three snow machines with Johnson riding on the backseat. Jackson drove to an area where the caribou were known to congregate this time of the year. Evidently, Johnson had no experience riding snow machines and fell off the sled and the group kept riding, leaving the boy to follow the tracks and catch up with the hunting party on foot.

"It was apparent that the boy was mad that the group left without him. Getting meat was the priority; it wasn't a guided hunt. Jackson probably felt little obligation to get the boy and risk losing the chance to harvest meat for their families. The event clearly strained the relationship of the boy and the other Kiana hunters," said Trooper Schuerch.

In court documents, Johnson said the blood and carnage on the snow—watching them gut and butcher the animals, including a cow that had an unborn calf in its womb—was overwhelming to him. "This baby never had a chance, you see, and Freddy was callous in not caring. It made me sick to my stomach," said Johnson.

The coroner testified that Freddy Jackson, age forty-three, received four bullet wounds: the upper left arm, the left buttocks, the left forearm, and a large wound in the right arm. It was the doctor's opinion that Jackson had bled to death. Clarence Arnold, age thirty-nine, suffered four bullet wounds: the upper arm, the side below the rib, the right hip, and one in the left wrist. There were also upper back and scalp lacerations. Arnold, like Jackson, bled to death. Oscar Henry, age sixty-four, had three wounds: one in the neck at the base of the skull, which killed him instantly, and one in the left leg and one in the right leg.

On March 11, 1971, a sentence of life imprisonment was handed down to Norman Leroy Johnson for the slaying of three Eskimo men during January of 1970. The sentence did provide for probation if the parole board found that Johnson was no longer a threat to society.

On June 15, 1973, the Supreme Court of Alaska heard in *Norman Leroy Johnson v. the State of Alaska* some of the following testimony:

A defense was mounted based on showing that, at the time of the slayings, Johnson was suffering from a mental disease or defect such that he was not responsible for his actions.

Dr. J. Ray Langdon testified that he had examined Norman and had reviewed the records of the investigation, some of Norman's previous medical history, as well as results of tests performed by a clinical psychologist. Dr. Langdon found that Norman was not, at the time of the examination, overtly psychotic or irrational, but that the tests and history showed evidence of severe mental illness, namely, a latent schizophrenic process which, if it became an overt psychosis, would most likely be of a paranoid or persecution type. Norman was in a totally unfamiliar situation, in the extremely cold Arctic wilderness, with three Eskimos, so his mental illness might have become overt. The doctor also testified that the emotion that would accompany the type of acute decomposition that Norman went through would be "primarily a panic."

Barbara Ure, another psychiatrist, also testified on Norman's behalf. On the basis of extensive interviews, Dr. Ure found evidence that Norman was a fetishist:

"The ego of the fetishist is what is involved in this killing, . . . he identified with the baby and the mother he lost—compromised his own body image which was already fairly well compromised, that is, he was insecure as to who he was, having lost contact with his culture, with his geography, he was pretty much displaced.

"These men would become the enemy, you see, and he—they—he could be killed by them just like this caribou was and this baby caribou . . . really it's the baby that never had a chance because this is Norman in a certain sense . . . who really never had a chance . . . Did not get up to urinate, he did have an erection, not a sexual sort of thing but in a sense of asserting his identity, preserving his survival and that it was totally incongruous to even consider the possibility of masturbating but then there's one other point that is when a fetishist cannot deny his identification with his mother, he generally does break down, you see, and so this is what I think did happen and that I do believe he did see the tent . . . and that his survival was threatened and that he doesn't know what he was doing and that he shot in self-defense."

Dr. John Rollins testified for the state of Alaska: "Norman showed no signs of mental disease, disorder, or defect that would preclude him from being able to conform to the law. Norman had the capacity to deliberate about the acts he was committing, particularly because of his ability to recall details of the events."

In 1974, Norman Leroy Johnson was released from the Federal Bureau of Prisons on a mental condition appeal in Lompoc, California. He later moved to Los Angeles, California.

In an interview for this book, Retired Colonel Tom Anderson gave extensive credit to the troopers who brought this murderer to justice. Bob Boatright had a difficult job keeping the community from turning on whites while getting the information he need to solve the crime. Without the help of Trooper Lorry Schuerch, the community would have exploded and who knows what could have happened and how many lives would have been lost or ruined. He brought several important pieces of evidence to the case and helped quickly establish the innocence of Clarence Wood. He truly brought a needed calm and reassured the locals that the troopers would do whatever it took to find the real killer.

Anderson also commented that the fact the troopers believed that an Eskimo couldn't have committed the crime helped establish a stronger rapport with native Alaskans.

Anderson said that Johnson's early release in 1974 was one of the more frustrating moments of their careers.

Dead Guy up the Tracks

It was August 1991 and Trooper Mike Sears was finishing his paperwork toward the end of a 2:00 p.m. to 10:00 p.m. shift. Twenty years earlier, the Talkeetna Post was located on the Parks Highway in what is today an organic food store sixteen miles from the village of Talkeetna. It was 9:55 p.m. when the radio from Palmer dispatch chimed with a report that a man had died on a trail up the Alaska Railroad tracks midway above Chase and below Curry, Alaska.

The trooper received a rail milepost number for the railroad track line and was told a service worker had picked up the deceased's relative. They were both waiting at the Talkeetna workstation and ready to assist in the body's recovery.

Sears immediately called his supervisor, Corporal Danny Sides, and caught him just before he was about to get in bed. The supervisor's home was thirty-five miles to the south in Willow. Sears asked whether the body could be recovered by a Fish and Wildlife Trooper in the morning.

"I don't think it's a good idea," said Sides. "As you know, that area is covered with grizzly bears and you know one will smell that body and have at it. The guy's poor brother-in-law is upset enough, we don't need him thinking we left his brother to rot on the trail and get eaten by a bear. Call the rail guy in Talkeetna, and I'll get up there with a four-wheeler in less than an hour to help you," he said.

Today, most rural trooper stations have a selection of ATVs and snow machines as part of their general transportation fleets.

However, back in the early nineties, unless the post was a true off-the-grid station without road access, the only troopers who had these machines were Wildlife Troopers.

Sears commented that the Talkeetna station at that time only had cruisers with Posi-traction and didn't even keep a four-wheel drive.

Trooper Sears reached the rail worker out of Talkeetna and he confirmed a train would not operate until around noon the next day. The train track service worker said that he had a brand new heavily modified six-passenger Ford F-250 that could drive on the rails. He was willing to make it available immediately for the thirty-mile trip up the tracks to recover the body. The worker also confirmed the body recovery could be made easier with an ATV to extract the deceased, whose body was roughly a mile and half up a steep trail. He noted that the deceased was a hefty man who weighed an easy 275 to 300 pounds.

The section out of Talkeetna north to Denali is called the Flag Stop Train and allows anyone to flag down a passenger train and be picked up along the designated line. Drop-offs can be arranged by the conductor when you board the train, with special stops easily made for cargo like water barrels, ATVs, appliances, and wood stoves. The passenger line serves as the only lifeline to many wilderness homesteads up the tracks out of Talkeetna. Homesteaders, hunters, recreational rafters, campers, and anglers use the rail line heavily almost daily in the summer and twice a week in the winter. This flag stop line is the last year-round flag rail line in North America. The Flag Stop Rail systems operated by the Alaska Railroad have been a necessary part of Alaskan life since its inception in 1903. Today, the rail line runs from Whittier to Anchorage and on through the rail belt to Fairbanks, traversing some of the most visually impactful scenery in the world.

While Corporal Sides was hauling the ATV up to the post, Sears contacted the coroner's office for permission to move the body. Based on an initial investigation, it seemed evident that the man had died of natural causes. If there was any sign of foul play at the scene, the extraction would be called off and a murder investigation would ensue.

By the time Sears and the corporal got the ATV in Talkeetna, it was 11:30 p.m. and the Ford was ready to load. They moved the small Honda ATV into the back bed, where it completely filled what was left in the cargo area because of all the toolboxes. Although summer is known for its midnight sun, by mid-August sunlight diminishes at a brisk five minutes a day. Typically, the sun sets near 10:30 p.m. and then rises close to 6:00 a.m.

The two troopers, the rail worker, and the deceased man's brother-in-law took more than an hour driving on the dark rail line. The route often followed alongside the Susitna River on the stretch to reach the trailhead of the homestead. The men wrestled the Honda out of the truck, dropped the bike with a springy thud on the tracks, and then headed up the trail to find the man.

As described by his brother-in-law, the man was found dead on the trail from the cabin and looked like he had died most likely of a heart attack. There were no signs of any suspicious evidence and everyone was relieved to find that a passing bear had not found the body.

Corporal Sides and the brother-in-law left to go to the cabin while Sears spent the next hour taking photos to document the scene. He meticulously noted any footprints along the trail and the state of the body in addition to the clothing worn and the personal items found on the deceased.

He determined that there was no suspicious trauma or any disturbance of the body other than the CPR performed by the brother-in-law. Sides joined Sears and he agreed that the story checked out after his separate interview with the brother-in-law and an inspection of the cabin. With all the photos inventoried and notes taken, it was time to move the body.

The brother-in-law, now with a large, odorous black malamute dog he brought from the cabin, said they had an old Ahkio military sled they used to slide heavy gear in the winter. The men agreed that the stout, plastic sled might be the best way to move the large, deceased Alaskan down the trail. With efforts to carefully bag up the man and do their best not to disturb the physical integrity of the deceased, the old homesteader was finally bagged, tied to the sled, and ready to travel down the trail.

The railroad worker had left the group when the investigation started to drive the Ford to a turnaround at Curry, almost twenty-five miles away. That left Corporal Sides on the ATV and the brother-in-law and Sears wrestling the Ahkio sled down the trail.

This was a serious challenge. The corporal was barely able to control the less than four-hundred-pound ATV plus the weight of the heavy man as both careened from side to side. The weight of the body pushed the sled precariously to the side of the hill. Sears weighed the scenario in his mind. Due to the weight proportions, he almost rolled the machine several times. If this kept up, it could potentially loosen the towrope and send the dead man down into the alder thickets below. Sears shook his head, quietly thinking, "It's never a 150-pound guy."

As Sears parked the sled safely at the tracks, the Ford arrived and was ready to pick up the group. The driver had shut the engine off and was standing outside the pickup in the dark. The conversation then turned to how the men would get the four-wheeler into the truck bed.

The operator of the Ford said, "I can lower the truck frame, it will make it a little easier." With the flick of the switch, the massive Ford lowered the frame down five inches. The four men picked up the front of the wheeler and shoved it into the back of the tight-fitting bed. Then, they rolled it forward and got the back wheels onto the tailgate. Once the ATV was secured to the toolboxes, it was clear there would be no room for the body in the back of the truck. The men didn't feel trying to make it all fit it was worth the risk; the body could be crushed by the cargo or disfigured by the toolboxes.

By now, everyone's eyes shifted back and forth from the body to the truck. Within moments, it became clear that the deceased would need to ride inside the cab. The only viable solution was for the dead man to sit in an upright position, seat belted, in the back seat next to the dog and Trooper Sears.

Despite the man's mass being close to the weight of the ATV, the four men pushed the body into a sitting position in the back seat and had him belted up in no time. Corporal Sides sat in the front with the living relative and the driver. Meanwhile, Sears was relegated to the back with the musty-smelling dog and the deceased. "Sides was my boss. I couldn't let him sit next to the body," Sears said. It was now around 4:00 a.m.

The rail worker had kept the truck low to the rails and was ready to raise the truck and engage the rail wheels. As the truck lifted, resetting on the steel wheels, Trooper Sears thought it sounded a bit strange.

"The truck really seemed to labor as the rail system engaged. But hey, it's this guy's truck, he must know how it works," remarked Sears.

But then even the driver commented quietly, "That didn't sound good." He moved the key forward to the start position. The engine in the Ford that the driver had owned for less than a week barely turned over with a single *chug*. It was followed by a notorious *click, click, click* sound.

It's unlikely the dog knew what had happened, but every living man in the cab knew the battery was stone cold dead.

"Oh, crap!" the driver said. "The old truck could go up and down with the engine off with no problem. . . ."

Sears really wanted to go home. In an effort to avoid spending one more second in the truck, he asked politely, "Isn't the train coming at noon?"

In reality, the train was not much of a solution, but a caution. In fact, the group could be in serious danger if they met an Alaskan Railroad train heading up the tracks at sixty miles per hour.

The driver said, "My radio will work here. I'll call dispatch and get the other guy who runs a truck out of bed to give us a jump. He'll do a check on the line around 9 to 10 a.m. It'll be ahead of the train, anyway, so we'll be okay."

The group would most likely not perish on the tracks in a fiery collision that morning; however, no one really wanted to spend any more time in the cab than they had to flanked by an ultra smelly dog, the deceased homesteader, and his dry cabin brother.

After a few minutes of talking about the truck's battery requirements, Sears said, "Hey, what about the battery in the ATV? Do you have any cables?"

The mood instantly improved with the hope that the tiny dry cell motorcycle battery in the ATV, which was the size of a human hand, could get the truck to start.

The driver headed for the toolbox to pull the twenty-foot cables. At this point, Trooper Sears, ready to do anything to get out of the cab, went for the ATV battery. In less than five minutes, they affixed the cable to the tiny fingernail-sized pole connections of the tiny ATV battery. In the interim, the four hopeful men waited in the wilderness while the driver got ready to turn the key. After a quick check to make sure nothing else was drawing power, like the lights or heater, he nervously turned the key.

"It seemed like an hour went by, and it was so painful to listen to," said Sears. The truck barely turned over once. It sounded as though it would not get a second roll of the engine when suddenly the 460 big block gas engine roared to life.

A sense of relief and calm came over everyone. The deceased's brother-in-law was comforted in knowing that the group would safely get back to Talkeetna within the next hour and a half.

It was 6:00 a.m. when the bedraggled group arrived in Talkeetna, and another hour before the coroner's truck arrived to take the brother. Sides said that Sears had done a great job and then took the ATV back to Willow. Sears stayed behind with the family member, the dog, and the body.

After the coroner's van left the freight station, Sears headed home. It was just a short five-mile drive south to his cabin. His wife, who was used to the trooper returning home at all hours, greeted him warmly with a smile and a kiss.

"Oh, wow . . . What's the smell?"

His wife insisted that no matter how tired the trooper was, he was taking a shower before getting into the bed.

When she raised the question about the smell for the second time, he replied, "It could be me, a dog, a dead guy, or all three."

The trooper then turned and headed toward the shower.

Last Days of Toll & Nading

During the writing of this book, two troopers lost their lives performing a rescue of an injured snow machiner, Carl Ober, near Larson Lake just twelve miles from my home in Talkeetna.

Talkeetna is the internationally recognized staging point for Denali, also known as Mount McKinley, North America's tallest peak. It is surrounded by low, rolling hills in a broad valley between the Alaska Range and the Talkeetna Mountains.

On March 30, 2013, the fifty-six-year-old Ober called 911 on his cell phone at 7:35 p.m. His snow machine had gone off the track into a ditch and he was stuck in the snow under a major power line, the Intertie that links Anchorage to Fairbanks. He said he'd bruised his ribs, but seemed more worried about becoming hypothermic.

After Ober made his 911 call, a Talkeetna trooper first tried to organize a ground rescue. There are several well-traveled snow machine trails running to the lake from the off the road system near Talkeetna, but the community lacks the organized, local snow machine rescue group common in many rural Alaska villages.

Troopers made a call to try to find a Talkeetna volunteer to go get Ober, but when that failed, "Helo-1 was approved to perform a search-and-rescue mission," said Public Safety Commissioner Joseph Masters.

A trooper's search-and-rescue coordinator called fifty-five-year-old veteran Alaska State Trooper Mel Nading at 8:19 p.m.

The pilot said he'd check the weather before accepting the mission, then called back to say he'd go.

Nading left Anchorage at 9:17 p.m., landed at Sunshine—near Talkeetna along the Parks Highway—to pick up forty-year-old Trooper Tage Toll at 9:42 p.m. Toll was a former fixed-wing pilot who agreed to act as a spotter.

Two witnesses ten miles southwest of Larson Lake reported rain and sleet when the helicopter flew overhead around 10:30 p.m. That changed to snow by 11 p.m., with the snow coming down like "a son of a gun," according to an interview related in a meteorological report by National Transportation Safety Board (NTSB) Investigator Paul Suffern.

Within twenty minutes, they found the snow machiner along the power line. The two troopers landed, picked up Ober, dug out his machine, and got back in the helicopter for the short flight to Sunshine, a community along the George Parks Highway south of Talkeetna. The troopers called ahead to request an ambulance meet them at Sunshine Tesoro truck stop when they returned with the injured man.

The return flight should have taken five minutes. Medics were waiting to treat Ober, the rescued fifty-six-year-old Talkeetna resident, at the stop off Parks Highway.

After picking up the injured resident just beyond Larson Lake, the Eurocopter AS 350 B3 crashed 5.6 miles east of Talkeetna. The helicopter is believed to have gone down shortly after 11 p.m. It was about that time Nading radioed that he had found Ober and was headed for Sunshine. He was not heard from again.

When he did not show up as expected, two Alaska Wildlife Troopers went out on snow machines to look for the helicopter and the 210th, 211th, and 212th rescue squadrons of the Alaska Air National Guard were notified.

Known as the "special forces" of US Search and Rescue, the men of the ANG found the helicopter about 9:30 the next morning—Easter morning. Two pararescuemen were lowered to the scene and confirmed there were no survivors. There was little evidence at the site due to an intense fire.

Body remains and the black box were recovered during the second site inspection the following day. Heat from the debris had delayed recovery efforts the day of the crash by Troopers and the Air National Guard. The black box was sent to NTSB Vehicle Recorders Laboratory in Washington, DC, for analysis. NTSB investigators were requested from out of state due to the close working relationship with the pilot and local Alaskan federal inspectors.

Nading was the primary pilot of Helo-1, having flown more than three thousand hours since he joined the Troopers in the year 2000. He had close relationships with all rural troopers in the field. He had flown countless high-risk missions to safely rescue civilians and support troopers in difficult-to-reach areas of Alaska.

Nading had more than eight thousand flight hours in a helicopter, the main operations report said. An observer from the Alaska Mountain Rescue Group who flew more than three hundred search-and-rescue missions with him described him as an excellent pilot who did not take risks flying in bad weather and turned around if the weather soured mid-flight. Numerous other people described Nading as careful, professional, safe, and committed to the rescue mission.

Some of his efforts are documented in this book from the perspective of the troopers who rode with him. He was highly respected as one of the most capable wilderness pilots on the planet. I had never met Trooper Nading, but his name was mentioned by almost everyone I interviewed for this project. Nading is survived by his wife, three daughters, and five granddaughters.

I had met Trooper Tage Toll during dinner at Mountain High Pizza Pie, a local pizzeria-bakery in the town of Talkeetna. I approached him about any stories that he may have had for the book. After ten minutes of throwing ideas around, he told me of a trip into the bush while he was stationed in Glennallen several years ago.

After some elaboration, he recalled having driven a snow machine sixty miles one way into the bush to check up on a trapper a family member was concerned about. He found the older gentlemen expired in his cabin, frozen solidly to the floor. Extracting the body from the winter wilderness cabin deep in the Copper River basin was not ideal restaurant banter. So, we agreed to talk within the next few weeks. That chance meeting took place just two weeks before his untimely death.

Toll had a wonderful reputation as a dedicated trooper with an enduring sense of humor. We never had our final interview. But in the short discussion I had with him, I found him engaging with an absolute love of his state and job. He had been with the Alaska State Troopers for ten years, previously serving with the Kansas Highway Patrol.

He is survived by his wife and three sons.

End of Watch

Three troopers and one civilian pilot employee died in the line of duty during the writing of this book. As one would expect, any type of law enforcement job is tethered to a high degree of risk. In the case of the Alaska State Troopers, it's not only the risk of working alone with little backup that can be dangerous; it's working in extreme weather and in challenging terrain that many consider to be an even greater threat.

Since 1964, the Troopers have lost sixteen officers and one civilian pilot. Nine were lost in aircraft accidents; six to gunfire; one to physical assault; one to exposure; and one to a heart attack.

The following is a list of these fallen officers and a brief description of the events of their passing during their last watch.

Officers Leroy Garvin Bohuslov and Gary George Wohlfeil

March 5, 1964

While conducting a caribou study near the village of Farewell, Alaska, northwest of the Alaska Range, the two McGrath-based wildlife officers perished when their Champion 150 aircraft crashed at noon on March 5, 1964.

It took four days and multiple airplanes from state agencies and the Civil Air Patrol to locate the wreckage. Bohuslov was thirty-eight, and Wohlfeil was twenty-one. Investigations showed that the aircraft experienced a structural failure, losing the wing and sending the plane into a nose dive.

Trooper Dennis Finbar Cronin
February 18, 1974

An undercover operative, Irish-born Cronin, age thirty-one, was the first law enforcement state trooper to die in the line of duty. The Anchorage-based officer volunteered to protect an informant during a deposition. The informant, Bernard Lono, had unknowingly obtained a firearm. He subsequently shot the officer, his girlfriend, and then himself. All three were pronounced dead on February 18, 1974.

Troopers Larry Robert Carr and Frank Stuart Rodman
December 11, 1974

While transporting a drowning victim's body on Kodiak Western Airlines Flight Number 91, the two troopers were killed when the plane crashed.

In addition to the troopers, the crew and two passengers also perished. The flight had taken off from Old Harbor on its way to Kodiak. The cause of the crash was never determined. Trooper Carr was twenty-three and Trooper Rodman was twenty-five.

Trooper Roland Edgar "Skip" Chevalier Jr.
April 3, 1982

While attempting to intervene in a domestic dispute between his brother-in-law, Robert McCann Jr., and his father-in-law, Robert McCann Sr., Trooper Skip Chevalier, age thirty-three, was shot and killed at his family's winter cabin.

During the trial, Robert McCann Jr. was acquitted, stating the event was an accident and that the shot was aimed at his father in self-defense. Robert McCann Sr. pleaded guilty to felony assault for shooting and fatally wounding his son.

Sgt. John David Stimson
January 14, 1983

Stimson, accompanied by civilian pilot Gary Wiltrout, was responding to a distress call from Kennedy Air Service pilot Gayle Ranney.

They boarded a Jet Ranger helicopter from Cordova and later sent a mayday message that they were experiencing an engine failure. The helicopter went down just two miles from Ranney's crash site.

Although both men initially survived the crash, weather delayed rescue attempts. Stimson died due to exposure. The Cordova Fish and Wildlife Trooper was forty-one years old.

Trooper Troy Lynn "Skip" Duncan
May 19, 1984

Termed an "End of the Roader," unemployed transient Michael Silka was accused of murdering six people, including his neighbor in the village of Manley Hot Springs.

The Fairbanks Post dispatched the SERT team via helicopter. While tracking the man down by air, the helicopter hovered over Silka, demanding his surrender. In an exchange of gunfire, Trooper Skip Duncan, age thirty-four, was shot in the neck. Silka was killed by return fire.

Sgt. Robert Lee Bittick
October 11, 1994

While piloting a 1940s-era Grumman Goose amphibious plane in poor visibility, Trooper Robert Bittick crashed into a mountainside on the Canadian border close to Haines, Alaska.

The crash also killed a passenger, Public Safety Deputy Commissioner Claude Swackhammer.

A motorist on the Alcan Highway discovered the wreckage, and the bodies were removed. The recovery team found the trooper with his hands still on the yoke. Bittick was fifty-one years old.

Trooper Bruce Alan Heck
January 10, 1997

A veteran trooper with twenty-one years of service, Trooper Heck was participating in a car chase that resulted in hand-to-hand combat with a career criminal that ended his life.

John Phillips was out on parole for one day when he robbed a store and then stole a cab. In pursuit, Heck chased Phillips in his cruiser to mile 156 of the Glenn Highway. He then tracked him on foot into a wooded area.

Trooper Bruce Alan Heck, age forty-three, died at the scene, two hundred yards from the road. The assisting officer arrested Phillips, and he was sentenced to 142 years in prison.

Sgt. David C. Churchill
September 16, 1998

One of the most important cases of Churchill's career is chronicled in the chapter titled "The Story of Amy Sue Patrick."

After spending more than a decade as an investigator, Trooper Churchill moved to the Wildlife side to spend more time in the woods instead of at the desk.

While checking a hunter on the side of a mountain on the Kenai Peninsula, Churchill, age fifty-one, suffered a heart attack and died on the mountain.

National Park Rangers performed CPR and evacuated the trooper by helicopter. He was pronounced dead on arrival at a nearby hospital.

Trooper Hans-Peter Roelle
November 24, 2001

Responding to a domestic assault where a woman had fled a moving vehicle, Trooper Roelle, age forty, followed the suspect, Ryan Andrews, to his home.

Once there, the trooper was cornered and shot in the head by Andrews. After fatally shooting the trooper, Andrews shot his two small children and then took his own life.

Trooper Tage Brandel Toll and Pilot Mel Nading
March 30, 2013

Assisting Pilot Mel Nading in a rescue of a snow machine accident at Larson Lake just north of Talkeetna, Trooper Toll and State Trooper Pilot Nading were killed in a helicopter crash.

The weather and visibility were poor. The helicopter exploded on impact with the ground. The crash also claimed the life of the rescued occupant.

Trooper Tage Brandel Toll was forty years old, and Department of Public Safety Pilot Mel Nading was fifty-five.

Sgt. Patrick Scott Johnson and Trooper Gabriel Rich
May 1, 2014

Troopers Johnson and Rich responded to a VPSO's request for backup in the remote village of Tanana.

The VPSO reported that a local, armed resident had threatened residents. Gunfire ensued, and the two troopers were allegedly shot by nineteen-year-old Tanana resident Nathanial "Sach" Kangas.

The case was still pending at the time of this writing. Sgt. Patrick Scott Johnson, age forty-four, and Trooper Gabriel Rich, age twenty-six, were both members of the Fairbanks Rural Unit.

Acronyms and General Alaskan Terms

An Alaskan Native: A member or descendant of any of the aboriginal peoples of Alaska.

Arctic Entry: An enclosed entry where people can remove heavy or soiled clothing and boots before entering the main part of a home.

ANCSA: The Native Claims Settlement Act, the legal process that helped designate the many native Alaskan Corporations. The companies are socialist corporate entities that are major players in land ownership, mining, oil exploration, hotel, and numerous other contract services.

Athabaskan: The original native habitants of the Interior including central, southern, and the mountain ranges of Alaska.

Borough: Alaska's answer to a county, which is often the size of a smaller state in the Lower 48.

Breakup: The time in the spring when all snow and ice finally melts away, sometimes all at once. It is sloppy all over the state for two to four weeks. For Alaskans, it means the end of winter and the beginning of warm weather.

Bug Dope or Bug Juice: Usually a spray with a percentage of Deet to repel mosquitos or no-seems. A necessity in late spring and early summer.

Bunny Boots: Large, clumsy white or black military surplus rubber boots that keep feet warm down to minus sixty-five degrees.

The Bush: Villages and terrain that can only be reached by boat or plane. By some accounts, this comprises more than 95 percent of the state.

Cabin Fever: When Alaskans feel cooped up from being inside too long during the winter.

Cache (Cash): An elevated food storage cabin, out of reach of animals particularly bears.

Cheechako: A newcomer or greenhorn. An individual who hasn't spent at least one winter in Alaska.

Denali: The Tanana Indian name for Mount McKinley, meaning "the high one." Mount McKinley National Park was renamed Denali National Park in 1980. Though the mountain retains the name Mount McKinley, most Alaskans refer to it as Denali or "the Mountain."

Devils Club: A large leaf plant that grows over all but the Arctic Regions of the state. It has thousands of fine sharp barbed thorns, hated by all.

Dip Netting: A subsistence style of sockeye salmon fishing for state residents or Alaska Native people. A large net on a long pole is dipped into a river in the path of migrating salmon.

Dry Cabin: A home or cabin that has no source of water or a bathroom. They are commonplace in rural Alaska.

Eskimo: Generally the term used for Alaskan coastal natives as opposed to natives of the interior, i.e., Athabaskan.

Frog Dawg: Wildlife Trooper.

Heater Plugs, Plug-in Block Heater: An electrical plug protruding from the grill of car or truck. Plug it into an outside outlet, at home or at a business, and it keeps your engine block warm so it can start in temperatures below zero.

Honey Bucket: A five-gallon bucket or metal pail usually with a toilet seat mounted to it, filled with sawdust. For use when it's below zero outside in a dry cabin.

Ice Fog: A dense, hanging winter fog of suspended ice particles.

Interior: The central part of Alaska, ranging north from the Alaska Range to the Brooks Range, and east to the

Canadian border. The area is about the size of Texas and home to 100,000 people of which the vast majority live in the Fairbanks area.

Inupiat: The northwest and northern coastal natives.

Lower 48: The forty-eight contiguous states.

Mukluk: A warm, waterproof boot usually knee high, made from various animal hides and fur.

Muskeg: A swampy or mossy bog; an accumulation of sphagnum moss, leaves, and decayed matter resembling peat that's common on the tundra and in south central Alaska.

Musher: A person who travels or races by dog sled.

Native Alaskan: Someone born in Alaska.

Outhouse: The place where you go to the bathroom when you live in a dry cabin. Note, there is often a Styrofoam seat.

Outside: Outside the state of Alaska.

Outsiders: Anyone not from Alaska.

Permafrost: Ground that is frozen year-round averaging two to five feet under the surface. Much of central, northern, and western Alaska permafrost has remained frozen for thousands of years.

Permanent Fund or PFD: Alaskan residents receive an annual check from the state's Permanent Dividend Fund, royalties generated from the sale of crude oil.

PJ's: Medics on the National Guard and Air Force helicopters.

SERT: Similar to SWAT teams, they are a highly trained police strike force used in high risk situations.

Sloper: An individual who works on the North Slope.

Snow Machine or Tin Dog: A snowmobile.

Sourdough: Anyone old to Alaska. An "old timer." A term coined in the Gold Rush era.

Subsistence Hunting or Fishing: This occurs throughout Alaska all year long and is central to the customs and traditions of many cultural groups in Alaska. For most rural Alaska residents, it is critical to their nutrition, food security, and economic stability.

Termination Dust: The first, light dusting of snow, on the mountains. It's a warning that heavy snow is often less than thirty days away and signals the end of summer.

VPO: Village Public Officer.

VPSO: Village Public Safety Officer.

Wheeler: ATV or four-wheeler.

Yupik: Generally Southwestern coastal natives that at the time of white contact had numbers of less than eighteen thousand.

Index

137

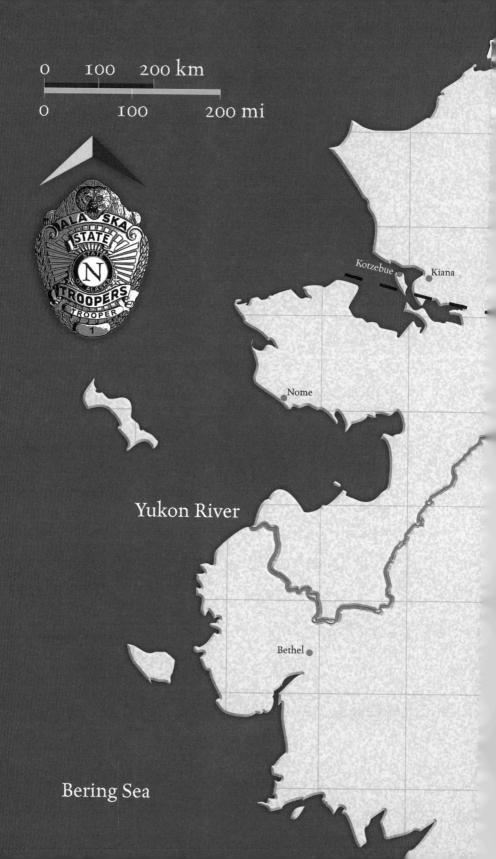

Kotzebue

Kiana

Nome

Yukon River

Bethel

Bering Sea

0   100   200 km

0   100   200 mi